People and Politics

Prentice-Hall International, Inc.
LONDON · TOKYO · SYDNEY · PARIS

Prentice-Hall of Canada, Ltd.

Prentice-Hall de Mexico, S.A.

PEOPLE

AND

POLITICS

An Analysis of the American Political System

Lewis A. Froman, Jr.
University of Wisconsin

Englewood Cliffs, N. J.
PRENTICE-HALL, INC.

LIBRARY OF CONGRESS
CATALOG CARD NUMBER 62–19402

PRINTED IN THE UNITED STATES OF AMERICA
65665—C

Current printing (last digit):

15 14 13 12 11 10 9 8

for my Mother and Father

PREFACE

The development of theory in any discipline is at the same time both important and difficult. It is important because theory helps us to explain why things happen the way they do, and to see relationships among phenomena that might otherwise be studied only separately and in isolation. Once we begin to see how many different factors are related to one another, and we acquire the ability to explain why and how things occur, we are then better able to exercise some control over these phenomena. This does not necessarily mean that we will be able to change things to suit our own purposes. Often theory shows us, in fact, how complicated the phenomena under study are and, because of interrelationships, how difficult it is to effect change. Theory does allow us, however, to understand how things happen and hence to be able to put such knowledge to use for our own benefit. Part of putting this knowledge to work is the ability to predict future states of affairs and then to take action to cope with the future in such a way that we can control its effects on us. Theory helps us, then, to understand the world around us and to calculate strategies and tactics for getting around in it.

Developing theory is also a difficult task. It involves organizing knowledge around a relatively few concepts, showing how the concepts are related to one another, and how the relationships, in turn, may be integrated into a logically interrelated set of hypotheses. It involves illustrating how the set of hypotheses helps to explain, relate, predict, and control. It involves, above all else, making generalizations which purport to organize and describe a wide range of phenomena. It is, in a nutshell, an attempt to make the complex simple.

This book is an attempt to develop a theory about politics. More particularly, it is an attempt to organize an interrelated set of hypotheses to explain American politics. It is hoped, however, that its utility will not end here. Theories are refined and become more universal as they are made to take into account more and more phenomena. The concepts and relationships found in this book may be useful for the explanation of politics in other than the American system. It is likely, however, that many of the generalizations would have to be modified. What this would amount to is showing that the generalizations herein operate or hold true only under particular conditions. As the conditions change, so do the generalizations.

Theory is always tentative. It is subject to the test of new evidence, to the solving of new problems, and to the exploration of new phenomena. Theory-building is an ongoing process of organizing large amounts of data. This book, then, is not a finished product. It is, rather, a step in the direction of understanding how the American political system functions—a large task that requires the combined efforts of many interested people.

A book of this nature owes much to the work of others. As it is an attempt to organize a large body of knowledge, I rely heavily on the research and thinking of colleagues in many disciplines. My gratitude to these people is duly recorded in the footnotes. I owe a special debt, however, to a number of colleagues who have either taught me a great deal and stimulated my thinking on the problems contained in this book, or who have read and criticized the manuscript in various forms before final draft, or both. The work of Professor Robert A. Dahl has been a constant source of ideas and stimulation. Professors Richard C. Snyder and Harold Guetzkow have also influenced my thinking considerably.

Professor Nelson W. Polsby, a close friend and an especially stimulating colleague, has done much to encourage me and to contribute to the writing of this book. To him I am especially grateful. James K. Skipper, Jr., Professors Jack W. Peltason, Murray Edelman, Ralph M. Goldman, Leon D. Epstein, Aaron Wildavsky, and my father, Professor Lewis A. Froman, have read and carefully criticized the entire manuscript. Many of their ideas have been incorporated into the present volume. My wife, Catherine A. Froman, also made considerable contributions to the writing of this manuscript.

In the final analysis, a book represents the work and thought of its author. I therefore accept full responsibility for any errors of omission or commission contained herein.

L. A. Froman, Jr.
Madison, Wisconsin

TABLE OF CONTENTS

People and Politics

1

POLITICS IN

EVERYDAY LIFE

Politics is a fascinating subject. Besides the considerable aid that a knowledge of politics obviously renders in understanding how government operates, it also gives us insight into how people behave. The study of politics involves us in the investigation of human beings interacting with each other, and as such it teaches us something about man, including ourselves.

But the study of politics, although an interesting topic by itself, also has practical application. We all have felt the desire, at one time or another, to influence the behavior of others. Perhaps we wanted a particular present for a birthday or other special occasion, and in various ways we attempted to let someone in a position to get us that present know that we wanted it. We could, for example, come right out and tell the other person what we wanted. Or we could, more indirectly, let a few hints drop over the dinner table that we were badly in need of whatever it was we wanted. Perhaps we engaged a third person to act as our intermediary to make it known to the prospective buyer-of-the-present that we desired the gift.

We might not have been consciously aware of it, but the technique we used to communicate our desire to the other person was probably determined, at least in part, by what we knew about him (or her), that is, how he (or she) would react to certain types of appeals. Perhaps we used a technique that had worked in the past and that we thought would work again. Or perhaps we tried to pattern our behavior after that of a sister or a brother whom we had observed to be successful in his attempts to secure what he wanted. In other words, we tended to "size up our man" and act accordingly. The child who asks his mother (who is a "soft touch" in this particular way) for money in the presence of others has no doubt been rewarded by many an ice-cream cone.

In the games that we play, we must make similar calculations if we wish to be successful. A poker player who does not learn the particular habits of his fellow players—for example, whether an opponent bluffs, or whether he is likely to be taken in by a bluff—is not likely to end the evening a very big winner. Similarly, a chess player who does not anticipate moves by his opponent and take them into consideration in his own moves will not become a very successful player. In any game that requires skill, knowing how your opponent plays and the moves he is likely to make is an extremely important part of your success in that game.

This, of course, assumes that you are playing to win. Many people seem not to. Those, for example, who want to make a good impression, who don't want to hurt others' feelings, who are sympathetic toward losers and feel guilty about winning, or who play "just for the fun of it" will often make it a point to refrain from winning, at least by a very big score. After all, life is a mixture of many games, all going on at once. Often it is quite "politic" to lose to the boss at golf, or to let baby brother win occasionally at ping-pong. But this is merely to say that the game at hand may not be the same for all the players.

Unfortunately, there are some kinds of games that affect everyone and that force each player to play to win. Perhaps it takes a situation in which loved ones are involved, or in which the prize is of high personal value. But whatever the situation, when the stakes are high, winning usually requires, among other things, a working knowledge of how the game is played.

One "game" in which the prize is often important is the determination of governmental policy. Perhaps the situation calls for dealing with a depression, or a war, or the rights of certain minority groups. We may think it very important that "our side" wins. But how do we play to win? How can we determine which actions on our part will be influential and which a waste of time? How do we learn to "size up our man"? We probably shall not know what actions are effective until we know the "rules of the game." The study of government is the study of a particular set of rules in a most intriguing sort of game. And generally the stakes are high.

Let's put this in slightly different language. We are speaking about how to be an effective citizen. If part of the definition of democracy is that "the people rule," we are addressing ourselves to the problem of how any of us, as citizens, can be effective in the ruling process. Knowledge of the political system is knowledge that can be put to work. When a governmental policy is important to us, if we understand the political system, we shall know how to act, using the "best" available alternatives open to us. This does not mean that knowledge of the rules of the game will inevitably lead to success. Winning involves more than knowledge concerning strategies and tactics. Such knowledge, however, is certainly helpful in playing the game. Besides helping us win, knowledge of the rules also provides us with the ability to calculate our chances of success or failure, so that we may avoid expending our energy and resources in games in which the probability of our winning is minimal.

A Definition of Politics

Politics, in its broadest sense, is concerned with the distribution of advantages and disadvantages among people. Individuals have different wants and needs. Since people are constantly interacting with each other, and since the satisfaction of many of a person's needs depends upon the relationships he establishes with others, the preferences of some individuals will inevitably come into opposition with the preferences of others. This opposition of preferences may result in competition or conflict and in attempts by those concerned to reach some sort of accommodation, varying from elimination of the competitor to a reconciliation of differences. How "payoffs" are distributed among the parties in conflict depends upon two very important factors: (1) the type of decision-making process, and (2) the people involved and the resources that they have available. We shall be dealing with both of these factors throughout this book. But no matter what kind of decision-making takes place—for example, bargaining, orders in a chain-of-command, or violence—or what kinds of people and resources are involved, the outcome may be described as a distribution of advantages and disadvantages among the parties to the dispute. For example, if a compromise is reached, perhaps all the parties involved in the controversy will be able to benefit. Often, however, some participants benefit more than others in the distribution of payoffs.

Let us, in this first chapter, give an exam   ow conflict resolution and the distribution of advantages   vantages are dependent upon both the type of decision-mak   cess and the people involved. One of the most important facto   uencing the distribution of outcomes is intensity.[1] Some of ou   references are not very intense, and so we let others have their w   . It is easier than arguing about a matter which we do not consider   ant. About other preferences, however, we feel very strongl   we want to have our way. Not only do different people have d   rent preferences, but the intensity of those preferences varies.

How intense people are in their prefe   ces often determines the distribution of outcomes in a dispute.   r example, we have all experienced a situation in which we were embers of a group (family, friends, or another person and ourselves)   nd the members of that group wanted to do something. Let us f   take a group in which everyone is approximately equal in status,   y, a group of friends. Let us assume that one of our preferences is to keep the group together. One-quarter of the group wants to see a movie and three-quarters would like to go to the local hangout. A discussion ensues and the decision made by the group is to go to the movies. What happened?

As political analysts, we are interested in why one-quarter of the group was able to get its preferences satisfied over the preferences of the other three-quarters. What occurred is what occurs in many relationships among people of equal status—some were more intense about their preferences than others and were less willing to give in. Whenever there is within a group a minority with strong preferences and a majority with weak preferences, and when one of the values of the group (especially among the majority) is to keep the group together, the result will be a decision in favor of the minority. That is, the minority's preferences about where they wanted to go were stronger

---

[1] See Robert A. Dahl, *A Preface to Democratic Theory* (Chicago: University of Chicago Press, 1956), Chap. 4, for an excellent and detailed treatment of the intensity problem in decision-making.

in relation to keeping the group together than were the preferences of the majority. Put another way, in relation to their own preferences about where to go, the minority felt less strongly about keeping the group together. They might even have threatened to pull out of the group if they didn't have their way. The majority, whose preferences about where they wanted to go were not so strong, felt more strongly about keeping the group together relative to this particular issue. They were not so willing to let the group dissolve into two groups if they couldn't have their way. In such a situation, those with the strongest preferences are likely to prevail.

Now let us contrast the above situation, in which the relationship among the participants was one of equality, to a military group in which the status of the participants is not equal (that is, generals have more authority than colonels, colonels more authority than majors, and so forth, all the way down to privates). What happens to the variable of intensity in this type of decision-making process? As we might expect, when a decision is to be made about what the army is going to do, the preferences of all the members are not given equal weight. Generals are more likely to have their way no matter how many soldiers are involved and no matter how strong the soldiers' preferences might be to stay in bed (or against keeping the group together!). The greater the inequality in status of group members, the less likely are preferences of the greatest number to prevail when in conflict with the preferences of the high-status members. As in the first example, inequalities in the distribution of advantages and disadvantages appear. But in the first case, the inequality was a result of the difference in the intensity of preferences; in the second case, there was a difference in rank of the persons involved as well as in intensity of preferences, and the former was more important than the latter in deciding the outcome.

A family situation offers another interesting example of the intensity problem. Generally speaking, parents have more authority in decisions which are made for the family than do children; that is, as in the case of the army, the preferences of all the members are not given equal weight. But often, as you might recognize in your own case, the preferences of the children will be taken into account, especially if they are expressed with some degree of intensity. Many parents are likely to give in to their children for the sake of family harmony, or because they love their children and feel that this is the way to make them happy. What is happening here is that a situation which could resemble the army in depending upon differences in authority has turned into a situation more like that of a group of friends in which everyone starts out approximately equal in authority and the most intense wins. This is only possible, however, if the parents choose to abdicate their inherently superior positions of authority in order to satisfy other preferences, for example, a quiet home or a happy family. In some families, children learn relatively early in life that they can change a situation in which authority is involved into one in which "friends" are involved and, hence, be able to have their own way.

The foregoing are three examples of political situations in which decisions were made affecting a group of people. The common thread running through them is that the preferences of some people on particular issues are being satisfied and the preferences of others are not. The distribution of payoffs depended upon who was able to influence the others, which, in turn, depended upon what kind of decision-making process was involved and how intense the participants were in their preferences.

Politics as Influence

Politics is concerned with (1) the decision-making process involved in the distribution of payoffs, and (2) what kinds of people receive what kinds of payoffs. Closely involved in this distribution of payoffs is the ability of people to influence other people. By definition, those who are more influential will gain a larger share of the advantages to be distributed. Those who are *potentially* more influential (who, for example, have more status, or larger material resources, or are more intense in their preferences) may or may not gain a larger share of the advantages to be distributed. This depends upon what kind of decision-making process is involved, and upon how these influential persons play the game.

Since influence is so important to a study of politics, a few words about it are in order. First, influence is defined as the ability to control the behavior of others.[2] Influence is a relational concept, that is,

---

[2] Robert A. Dahl, "The Concept of Power," *Behavioral Science*, vol. 2 (July, 1957), pp. 201–215, and Herbert A. Simon, "Notes on the Observation and Measurement of Political Power," *The Journal of Politics*, vol. 15 (November, 1953), pp. 500–516.

it involves at least two people. Potential influence consists of those factors that are correlated with actual influence and involves the resources that a person has at his disposal in his interactions with others and that make it easy or difficult for him to exercise influence. These factors or resources vary widely in situations involving influence and include such things as money, status, authority, intensity of preferences, number of people on your side, and so forth.

Second, influence need not be a conscious attempt by one person to control the behavior of others. That is, a person need not intend to influence others in order to do so. In fact, much of the influence we have with other people is totally unknown to us. Perhaps someone likes us and wants to be like us. That person begins to imitate the way we behave. We are influencing his behavior without our even knowing it. Perhaps we have strong preferences about something and as a result we get our way. We may not consciously be trying to win— it just comes out that way as we express our preferences. The most successful influencers of people, however, are probably conscious of much of their influence. In fact, they may consciously try to manipulate people in hopes that the latter will act in the desired manner. Involved in this conscious use of influence is knowledge of the interaction situation, what techniques of persuasion are successful with certain kinds of people, how intense others are about their preferences, and so forth.

Before we jump to any conclusions, we should observe that the conscious use of techniques in order to win is not necessarily "evil." The assignment of "good" or "bad" is determined, at least in part, by the content of the decision and the consequences it has for others. Let us not confuse, as so many people do, the process by which the decision is made with the decision itself. Both the process of decision-making and the content of the decision may be evaluated independently. These two evaluations depend upon a number of factors, but certainly our preferences as to process and content have a great deal to do with our evaluations. For example, to revert to an earlier illustration, perhaps the soldiers in the army who had been consciously manipulated by their officers when once on the battlefield began to be grateful that they had been forced to learn how to shoot a rifle, even if it meant getting up at five o'clock in the morning.

Whether decisions are "good" or "bad" is also partly determined by other values that people may have. If violence is employed as a conscious technique in persuading others to do our bidding, this is generally considered "bad," but only in certain circumstances. In war, violence is considered necessary to win. In this case the consequences which may result if violence is not used are more dreaded than the actual use of force. Violence becomes appropriate for many people when they are intense about their preferences, when they are in conflict with others who are also intense about their preferences, and when they can find no other way to solve their differences.

There are two common errors that we all make by confusing, in our evaluation of decisions, the process by which decisions are made with the content of the decision. First, if we disapprove of the content of the decision, we often place this discontent upon the decision-making process. For example, if Congress passes a law with which we are in disagreement, we may attribute the result to a small group of selfish men who were able to work their will on the majority. But when Congress passes a law with which we are in agreement, we attribute this to the workings of democracy and majority rule or the actions of enlightened statesmen acting in the national interest.

Second—just the reverse of the above—when we approve of the content of the decision, we are likely, no matter what the decision-making process, to suggest that the "end justifies the means." We are likely to blind ourselves to the possibility that the same decision might have been reached through a process which we hold in greater approval. Either way, we are making an error of judgment based on our inability to see process and content as being different, an error of which politicians are well aware and which they use to their own advantage. Many a congressman, be he Democrat or Republican, will suggest to his constituents that certain "selfish interests" on the side of the opposition are the "cause" of the defeat of legislation in his constituents' interests. He will rant and rave about unfair tactics on the part of the opposition and attribute the defeat solely to their obstructionist tactics. In this instance the politician is suggesting that the process of decision-making, a process of which he probably approves when he is on the winning side, is "bad" because the decision is "bad." And many in the American public accept this argument.

The intentional use of certain techniques of persuasion and influence is not "good" or "bad" *per se.* We all consciously try to manipulate the behavior of others when we consider it important to do so. The mark of a successful politician is his ability to satisfy his strong preferences without jeopardizing his chances for satisfying preferences that he may have at a later time. To do so requires that he know the "rules of the game"—when they can be broken and when they must be adhered to—and his chances of success in employing given techniques. The most effective manner in which people may counter those with strong preferences with whom they disagree is to get into the game. Raving about injustice will be less effective in satisfying your preference for what *you* consider just than to engage actively in pursuing your preferences. Otherwise you withdraw from the game and leave the spoils for those who do attempt to satisfy their preferences. Such participation requires that you, too, know the rules of the game and how consciously to achieve what you are after.

There is nothing inherently "dirty" or "evil" about playing politics. Generally, those who consider politics to be "dirty" are one of two kinds of people. Either they have not, as yet, developed strong preferences themselves about one choice over another, or they have developed strong preferences but constantly lose. The former group of people cannot expect those who *have* developed strong preferences to act as though their preferences were weak. Many moralizers in politics are among those who, because their preferences are not clear to themselves, rail against the *methods* employed by those whose preferences are clear. Moralizers, in this sense, withdraw from the game because outcomes are not important to them. They prefer, rather, to discuss the procedures of playing as though there were something inherently "evil" about them. This is simply a rather simple-minded substitute for trying to understand *why* things happen the way they do and hence impedes insight into possible strategies for changing the system. The latter group, who have strong preferences but constantly lose in politics, become moralizers primarily because their views have not gained enough support among others to prevail. Their moralizing may be directly attributed to a behavior syndrome known as "sour grapes."

The Politics of Government

Our definition of politics as the distribution of advantages and disadvantages among people is obviously a very broad one. That is, it includes more than just government. In a sense, we are all politicians and we play politics every day of our lives. We are constantly attempting to satisfy our preferences, and we often run into conflict with others in the process. Many of us, when conflict occurs, withdraw our preferences in favor of those of others. However, when our preferences are held intensely, the situation becomes "important" and, if we wish to be successful, we have to learn to "play the game."

Our definition of politics does not, however, take into account all human behavior. We are interested in those situations in which advantages and disadvantages are being distributed, that is, in which preferences are being satisfied and denied, among people. Excluded from our discussion are certain "individual" acts, like brushing one's teeth or day-dreaming. The behavior we are interested in is that which affects other people. Brushing one's teeth might result in an engaging smile which could be an asset in our ability to influence others, but we are more interested in the situations in which a smile is flashed than in the brushing of teeth.

Some decisions to distribute advantages and disadvantages are obviously more important than others. Generally, decisions become more significant as they affect more people. Although all behavior which influences the distribution of advantages and disadvantages is political, the larger the number of people such behavior influences, the more significant and important it becomes. Decisions which influence communities, states, and whole societies are therefore of utmost concern. Because so many people are affected, the study of governmental decision-making may be justified on this basis alone.

But the number of people involved is not the only criterion by which we judge the importance of decisions. Decisions also increase in significance as the payoffs increase in amount, as they embrace a wider range of values, as people value them more intensely, and as distributions become more binding and irreversible. We can say, however, that the number of people involved distinguishes governmental from most other decisions, or at least distinguishes the traditional focus of the political scientist.

Government is the authority established to settle disputes and to distribute many kinds of advantages and disadvantages within the particular group involved, be it a small community or a whole nation. Generally speaking, only those problems which cannot be settled (or are not settled) by people themselves reach the government for decision. Hence, they are likely to be problems of extreme importance. Often the reason they could not be settled outside of government is that the parties involved in the controversy are intense about their preferences, and none is willing to give in to the others. In order to avoid violent resolution of their differences, government authority is called upon to mediate in the dispute. If the government is considered legitimate,[3] its decision will be accepted, at least temporarily, by the parties involved in the controversy.

However, government is not an impartial mediator. That is, it is not an organ established by society to keep aloof from the controversy and merely pass on the "merits" of the case before it. Like the so-called "independent voter" who listens to the arguments of all sides and then "rationally" makes his choice, government by an impartial set of decision-makers is a myth. Government is an authority established to settle conflicts, and parties to conflicts (especially those who feel intensely) are likely to try to influence the decision in their own favor. In fact, this is one acceptable definition of government: the implementation of the preferences of people into public policy.

But which people are listened to? Whose preferences are translated into public policy? Much of this book is directly concerned with an answer to these questions. Let us, for the moment, merely sketch out a partial answer.

Elected politicians gain office from the votes of a certain number of people, geographically defined. They owe their election to the votes, campaign funds, party work, and efforts of those who elected them. Politicians must face a new election periodically. This means that if certain preferences within their constituencies are not satisfied, they may not be able to count on the continued support of those who helped them in the past. Generally speaking, politicians, for a variety of reasons, enjoy their work and desire to remain in office.[4] Hence they must pay attention to those who played a role in putting them there. And the stronger the support, the greater the obligation by the politician to the supporters.

Elected politicians, then, are not impartial observers of controversy,

---

3 Seymour M. Lipset, in his *Political Man* (Garden City, N. Y.: Doubleday & Co., Inc., 1960), Chap. 3, discusses the concept of legitimacy as it relates to governmental systems. See also Herbert A. Simon, *Administrative Behavior* (New York: The Macmillan Company, 1947), on "zones of legitimacy."

4 See Stimson Bullitt, *To Be a Politician* (Garden City, N. Y.: Doubleday & Co., Inc., 1959), especially Chap. 2, for a discussion of this point.

but partisan participants in controversy, especially where the interests of their constituents are involved. This is what we mean when we say that our elected officials are responsible to the people: we mean that they are responsible to *some* of the people, and especially those people who make their preferences known and consciously attempt to control policy outcomes by influencing governmental decision-makers.

Our whole governmental structure is made up of people who owe their positions to others—appointed officers as well as elected government officials. There are certain minimum requirements which must be met if they are to continue in office. Their allegiance, however, is not due to only one group of people.[5] Generally, they owe their allegiance to a number of groups within their constituencies. Take a "typical" congressman, for example. Perhaps certain ethnic groups aided in this election. Labor, business, farm, veterans, or civic groups may also have played a part. In order to gain and hold their support, the congressman finds it necessary to make certain promises to these people. He must, at the minimum, promise that he will have their interests at heart in any controversy which comes before him.

This, in fact, is one of the aspects of politics which makes it so fascinating. People who are accountable in their positions to others find it necessary to calculate the effect of their actions on those to whom they are held accountable. There are certain risks in making a decision because it involves people engaged in controversy, and obviously a decision cannot completely satisfy everyone. Politicians must calculate their gains and costs before arriving at their decisions. This is indeed a precarious business, especially when the possibility of losing office hangs in the balance.

Our government, then, considers the interests of those who helped elect its members. We would probably not want to have it any other way. But it is also a fact of politics that those people who are organized, who are intense about their preferences, who make their preferences known persistently, who know to whom to make their preferences known and what kinds of techniques are appropriate in given situations are likely to be the most successful. Hence, advantages and disadvantages are distributed somewhat unequally among the popula-

---

[5] Richard E. Neustadt, in his *Presidential Power* (New York: John Wiley & Sons, Inc., 1960), discusses the question of multiple loyalties of office-holders, especially with respect to those political appointees who are accountable to the President.

tion, depending upon the zeal, skill, diligence, and other resources of those who express their preferences. Obviously, if a group wants its preferences known and acted upon, it is necessary to talk—persistently and to a number of people. Since governmental power in the United States is diffused among many actors, such as congressmen, the President, various governmental agencies, and the courts, the more people you are able to influence, the more likely you are to be successful in achieving your preferences, assuming equality of power among those being influenced. Since there is also a great disparity in the amount of authority which different government officials have on various issues, it is also a worthwhile strategy to concentrate your attention on those with the most authority on any given issue.

Because governmental decisions affect a large number of people, and because most decisions that are made will affect at least a segment of the population that feels intensely about its preferences, they are significant and important to study. But this, as we have already mentioned, is not the only criterion of importance that can be established. Some decisions are more important than others even when the same number of people are affected. A decision by the government to raise taxes and a decision to go to war both affect approximately the same number of people, but in different ways. Hence, another criterion of importance is the way in which the decision affects people, including the size of the payoff, the range of values involved, the intensity of feeling, and how binding the decision is on their lives.

To illustrate, certain decisions involve people in situations of greater risk than others. They may involve people in situations which require a great deal of their time and energy, or they may concern preferences about which a great many people feel strongly. Generally speaking, the greater the cost involved to a number of people, the higher the payoff, the more intense the preferences, and the more binding the decision, the more significant it is. All of these are the implicit criteria which political scientists use in deciding what problems are important to study. Many of these decisions involve government, but not all. For example, disputes between labor and management are almost always significant by the above criteria. They are political decisions and fitting for study by political scientists (as well as by others, of course, who may be interested).

Hence, political scientists are interested in analyzing a wide range of decisions, but traditionally they have centered their attention on governmental decisions.[6] And for a good reason. Most governmental decisions do affect large numbers of people and do consume many people's time and energy and do arouse strong preferences. Some, however, do not (for example, private bills in Congress affecting only particular, named people). And some decisions outside the formal apparatus of government are also significant by our criteria. The important point, however, is that all are political decisions, that is, all involve the distribution of advantages and disadvantages among people with different resources. Our task is to see how people convert resources into influence, how the play of influence and counter-influence determines outcomes, and how outcomes distribute payoffs to various citizens and groups. This is the study of politics.

---

[6] See David Easton, *The Political System* (New York: Alfred A. Knopf, Inc., 1953); Charles S. Hyneman, *The Study of Politics* (Urbana: University of Illinois Press, 1959); and Vernon Van Dyke, *Political Science: A Philosophical Analysis* (Stanford: Stanford University Press, 1960), for further discussions of the kinds of questions that political scientists study.

2

THE INDIVIDUAL

AND POLITICS

Politics is concerned with the behavior of individuals and groups as they vie for a favorable distribution of advantages. As individuals and groups come into conflict over their preferences, many attempt to satisfy their preferences at the cost of others.

One of the functions of government is to keep these conflicts from becoming violent. The politics of public government is much like other kinds of politics except that governmental decisions are made on behalf of people within a particular geographically and legally defined area by a set of (more or less) responsible decision-makers. The study of governmental politics is, in large measure, the study of the process by which these decision-makers decide on one alternative as opposed to another and of the distribution of payoffs resulting from their choices. By "process" is meant not only the behavior of the decision-makers, but also the behavior of those who attempt to influence their decisions. Hence, our perspective of "how government works" is considerably broadened to include the study of a great deal of human behavior outside of government itself but which is, nevertheless, relevant to the decision-making of formal leaders.

Since we are interested in the behavior of people (whether singly or in groups), we may ask ourselves the question: "What do we know about people and how they behave which will help us in understanding their political behavior?" This chapter is concerned with the behavior of individuals; in the next chapter we shall discuss the behavior of groups.

Normative and Empirical Theories of Man

There are, of course, many ways in which one may attempt to "explain" human behavior. For example, it used to be thought, and some people still believe, that the behavior of individuals is determined by the activity of spirits. "Evil" people (that is, those people who violate the generally accepted standards of how people should behave in the society) are considered to be under the influence of "evil" spirits; "good" people (that is, those who follow the generally accepted standards of how people should behave in the society) are considered to be under the influence of "good" spirits. Much religious thought has been devoted to the study of various kinds of spirits and the consequences for human behavior which result from being under the influence of one type of spirit as opposed to another. Various methods were devised to propitiate these spirits and to attempt to exert some control over them, for example, prayer, sacrifice, and other rituals. Great controversies ensued over whether man was born "evil" and had to atone for this "evilness" through the use of a number of rituals, or whether man was born "good" and merely had to be careful not to fall into the many pitfalls and traps which the "evil" spirits would set for him during the course of his life.

This kind of explanation of human behavior we shall call *normative* theory. It relates to the kinds of questions about what man "should" or "ought" to do in order to lead the "good" life. Normative theorists include religious leaders, theologians, certain kinds of philosophers (for example, Confucius, Plato, Aristotle, Rousseau, and Mill), moralists, and others who attempt to determine the "proper" behavior for man that will lead to the "good" life and perhaps, in some religions, a "heavenly" life after death.

There is, however, another manner in which the study of man may be approached. We shall call this *empirical* theory. Its primary focus is on an explanation of how man, in fact, *does* behave rather than how he should or ought to behave. Empirical theorists attempt to determine, with as few unproven assumptions as possible, factors which help to explain man's activities on this earth. They do this with the following criterion as a guide: that any explanation which is given may be verified in principle through the use of man's sense apparatus (the five senses of seeing, smelling, hearing, touching, and tasting), without relying on a "sixth" sense.[1]

This particular kind of study also has its rituals, primarily employed to satisfy the criterion of verifiability just mentioned, that is, the ability to show, by the use of the senses, that what is stated to be the case is the case and that others, using the same procedures, may replicate or reproduce the results. We usually associate empirical theory with natural and physical scientists who carry on research investigating "nature." But empirical research need not be confined to the study of our environment. There is also the study of man by social scientists using rituals appropriate to such study and based on similar reasoning, logic, and dependence on the criterion of verifiability as are found in the natural and physical sciences. This is not to suggest that social scientists are in any way attempting to emulate or imitate natural and physical scientists. Each discipline has its own peculiar problems and methodology. It is to suggest, however, that empirical theorists, whether they study man or his environment, do share a philosophy of science and criteria for establishing knowledge.[2]

"Truths" (true statements) are said to be established in empirical theory when there is a high degree of correspondence between statements made about the world and the results of experiments and research which are designed to verify the statements. The ability to predict behavior in the future (whether it is the behavior of molecules or the behavior of men) is central to the demonstration of true statements. If one can predict future behavior, this is strong support that the concepts one employs in explanation have a high degree of utility

---

[1] For a discussion of the principle of verifiability, see Alfred J. Ayer, *Language, Truth and Logic* (New York: Dover Publications, Inc., n.d.); Arnold Brecht, *Political Theory* (Princeton: Princeton University Press, 1959); and Hans Reichenbach, *The Rise of Scientific Philosophy* (Berkeley: University of California Press, 1951).

[2] For introductions into the philosophy of science, see Reichenbach, *The Rise of Scientific Philosophy;* John G. Kemeny, *A Philosopher Looks at Science* (New York: D. Van Nostrand and Co., 1959); and Gustav Bergmann, *Philosophy of Science* (Madison: University of Wisconsin Press, 1957).

and that statements using these concepts are true.[3] Empirical theorists include social scientists (for example, psychologists, sociologists, and anthropologists) and others interested in the investigation and explanation of man's behavior using the verifiability criterion.

The primary distinction between normative and empirical theorists is that the former are interested in asking and answering *should* and *ought* questions, whereas the latter are interested in asking and answering *is* questions. Our task in this book is not to ask and answer the question: What should the political relations of men be? Rather, our task is to ask and answer the question: What are the political relations of man? Hence, the explanation of human behavior to follow will be in the tradition of empirical theory rather than of normative theory.

An Empirical Theory of Human Behavior

People behave on the basis of certain values, beliefs, and attitudes which they have concerning the world around them. This section will be concerned with explicating what is meant by *values, beliefs,* and *attitudes* and will develop propositions showing how these concepts are related to one another.

A *value* is a statement of "good" or "bad," "right" or "wrong," something which is desired or thought desirable.[4] All of us have developed a set of values. These values may be about things as "unimportant" as personal tastes in food or clothing; or they may be about how we think others should behave. We may feel, for example, that all men should be treated equally, or that the system of free enterprise should be preserved. These latter values are more "important" than personal tastes by the same criterion that made certain political decisions more important than others (discussed in the previous chapter); that is, the number of people who are affected by our

---

[3] See, for example, Herbert Feigl, "Notes On Causality," in Herbert Feigl and May Brodbeck, eds., *Readings in the Philosophy of Science* (New York: Appleton-Century-Crofts, Inc., 1953), pp. 408–418.

[4] For a more lengthy discussion of values, see Lewis W. Beck, *Philosophic Inquiry* (Englewood Cliffs, N. J.: Prentice-Hall, Inc., 1952); Ralph B. Perry, *Realms of Value* (Cambridge: Harvard University Press, 1954); and Charles Morris, *Varieties of Human Value* (Chicago: University of Chicago Press, 1956).

values. Generally speaking, those values which involve a greater number of people are more important. Other criteria of importance mentioned in Chapter 1 are also relevant here—that is, the risk involved in pursuing one's values, the time and energy involved in pursuing one's values, and, of course, the intensity with which values are held. The more intense our values, the more important they are to us, and the more likely we are to act on them, all other things being equal.

Values may be of three kinds. First, the desired, that is, a person's wants and needs. For example, "I want an apple," and "I want people to be honest," are statements which indicate that the individual places a value on the object to which the statement refers. Second is the desirable. This is the common meaning of *values* and involves "should" or "ought" questions. For example, "Nations should live in peace," and "The United States should have a comprehensive social security system," are both value statements indicating a desirable state of affairs envisioned by the person making the statements. Religious and moral values are also states of affairs perceived as desirable by many people. A third kind of value statement is a statement involving a relationship of means to an end. For example, I may place a value on medicine because it is perceived by me to contribute to the restoration of my good health, even though it may not taste good or fit into the scheme of things which I consider to be inherently desirable.

Beliefs are statements which we use to describe our environment. Beliefs are of two kinds: beliefs *in* something, for example, belief in God, or belief in Santa Claus; and beliefs *about* something, for example, a belief that the world is round (or pear-shaped, or flat), or a belief that governmental politics is no more corrupt than any other form of politics. Statements of belief *in* something are not subject to empirical proof. They are matters of "faith." Statements of belief *about* something are subject to empirical proof and are the kinds of beliefs about which we shall be speaking. As with values, some beliefs are more "important" than others, depending upon the number of people who are affected by the belief. That is, a belief that Johnny Jones is inferior is less important politically than a belief that Negroes are inferior. Beliefs, of course, have the additional significance of being either true or false.[5]

---

[5] For a more detailed treatment of beliefs, see Milton Rokeach, *The Open and Closed Mind* (New York: Basic Books, Inc., 1960).

Also, beliefs *about* something are of two kinds. The first type of belief is that about which there is controversy, that is, low agreement about the validity of the belief. People may disagree about the "truth" of a belief for many reasons, but two important ones are: (a) not enough evidence in support of the belief (or the existence of contrary evidence), and (b) the belief is empirically "fuzzy," that is, the *meaning* of the belief statement is not clear. (We shall have occasion to come back to this later in this chapter.) The second kind of belief about something is called a "fact," about which there is little or no disagreement or controversy concerning its validity. In other words, a fact is a verified empirical belief about which there is strong agreement that it is true.

An *attitude* is a predisposition of an individual to evaluate some aspect of his world in a favorable or unfavorable manner, that is, a predisposition to approve or disapprove, like or dislike, some social or physical object.[6] Attitudes may be thought of as having two components. The first is an *affective* component, consisting of feelings of like and dislike which may vary in *direction* of feeling and *intensity* of feeling. The second component of attitudes is the *cognitive* or belief component. These are statements which describe the object of the attitude. In other words, attitudes are made up of feelings (affective component) and reasons (beliefs) why the person feels the way he does.[7]

We all have attitudes about a great many objects and relationships in our environment. Attitudes aid us in coping with our environment and in handling the many complex and different situations with which we are daily confronted. In doing this, attitudes may serve four functions for the individual: [8]

1. *Utilitarian function.* Attitudes aid us in achieving our values. That is, if one of my goals is to become a politician, then developing a favorable attitude toward members of my political party will probably aid me in achieving my goal. An unfavorable attitude toward

---

[6] The literature on attitudes is voluminous. For an excellent summary, see Bert F. Green, "Attitude Measurement," in Gardner Lindzey, ed., *The Handbook of Social Psychology* (Reading, Mass.: Addison-Wesley Publishing Co., Inc., 1954), vol. 1, pp. 335–370.

[7] See Daniel Katz, "The Functional Approach to the Study of Attitudes," *Public Opinion Quarterly,* vol. 24 (Summer, 1960), pp. 163–205, and Milton J. Rosenberg, "A Structural Theory of Attitude Dynamics," *Public Opinion Quarterly,* vol. 24 (Summer, 1960), pp. 319–341.

[8] Katz, "The Functional Approach . . .," pp. 170 ff.

members of my political party, if expressed often enough, will probably hinder my ambition.

2. *Knowledge function.* Attitudes serve as a means by which an individual can organize his environment. That is, attitudes serve as economizing devices which allow us to react to familiar physical and social objects without having to think much about them. They serve as a way of economically organizing our knowledge and reactions to our complex environment.

3. *Ego-defensive function.* Attitudes serve the function of protecting the individual from certain kinds of situations which may be threatening to him. For example, an individual may feel threatened when in the presence of someone whom he views as being more intelligent than himself. An attitude of dislike for that person serves as a protective shell, a rationale for avoiding the other person's company and for refusing to put much weight on what he has said.

4. *Value-expressive function.* Attitudes serve as a means by which an individual may express himself and show other people what kind of a person he is. For example, Democrats who value their party very highly may want to express themselves by taking positions on a great number of issues. Their expressions of like and dislike on these issues serve to tell other people what they are like and how they feel about certain aspects of their environment.

If it were not for attitudes, an individual would feel quite lost in his environment. He would have no basis upon which to orient himself toward social and physical objects. He would have no habits of response. He would feel unprotected and threatened by his environment, as he would not know how to respond to it. Hence, attitudes are a major portion of a person's personality. It is through the expression of a person's attitudes that we learn something about him, his needs and wants, his values, his personal tastes, and his prejudices. We shall also learn something about his *political* behavior, a point that will be stressed in later chapters.

Values, beliefs, and attitudes do not stand in isolation to one another. They are related in a number of interesting ways.[9] Attitudes

---

[9] M. Brewster Smith, Jerome S. Bruner, and Robert W. White, *Opinions and Personality* (New York: John Wiley & Sons, Inc., 1956); Talcott Parsons and Edward A. Shils, *Toward a General Theory of Action* (Cambridge: Harvard University Press, 1951); and Milton J. Rosenberg, Carl I. Hovland, William J. McGuire, Robert P. Abelson, and Jack W. Brehm, *Attitude Organization and Change* (New Haven: Yale University Press, 1960).

may be said to be the product or the result of certain combinations of values and beliefs. For example, one of our values might be that "Equal representation of all interests within the United States is good." Further, we may believe that "Congress allows for equal representation of all interests within the United States." On the basis of this value-and-belief combination, assuming all else to be equal, we would predict a favorable attitude toward Congress; that is, we would predict that the individual holding this value and belief also will approve of Congress.

If it could be shown empirically that Congress does not in fact allow for equal representation of all interests within the United States (that is, if the belief upon which the attitude is based is shown to be false), it might be the case that one would change his attitude toward Congress. That is, because a person values equal representation, and he learns that Congress does not provide for such equal representation, the person may change his attitude from "I approve of Congress" to "I disapprove of Congress." It is also possible, however, that one would say, "Even if it is proved false that Congress allows for equal representation of all interests within the United States, I like it anyway," or "I like it for some other reason." In the former case, it is likely that the attitude would be serving some function for the individual other than a knowledge function (which is only one of the four possible functions mentioned earlier). He seems resistant to change, even if his beliefs are shown to be false. Many of our prejudices (which are, of course, attitudes) are of this nature. We are inclined to dislike certain things or people not really because of what we know or don't know about them, but because it helps us to work off our own inner tensions and frustrations. Such objects in our environment act as "scapegoats" for our own internal psychological problems. Information becomes irrelevant to changing these attitudes. On the other hand, we often hold our attitudes on the basis of many values and beliefs. Because we show that one belief is false does not necessarily mean that a person will change his attitude. It may be necessary to challenge a number of his beliefs before he will change his mind.

To recapitulate, often our attitudes are based on belief statements concerning things, events, consequences, and so forth, in the real world which are empirical statements and hence capable of being proved true or false (except attitudes, such as prejudices, which seem to be fulfilling certain "irrational" needs for the individual). We also often place a value on what these beliefs are about and say that we "like" certain things (both our beliefs and our "likes" and "dislikes" making up our attitudes) because they are instrumental in achieving our values. The interplay between values, beliefs, and attitudes is evident. If our beliefs turn out to be false, it may very well lead us to change our attitudes. Diagrammed, the relationship would look like this:

Value	*Belief*	*Attitude*
Equal representation of all interests within the United States is good.	Congress allows for equal representation of all interests within the United States.	I like Congress.

Put in syllogistic form:

Equal representation of all interests within the United States is good.
Congress allows for equal representation of all interests within the United States.

.·. I like Congress.

Technically, the above is not a valid syllogistic argument for the reason given above; that is, one could agree or disagree with the conclusion on the basis of other values and beliefs. The qualification "other things being equal" must be added. Attitudes such as "I like Congress" are usually based on a number of interrelated values and beliefs. For example, values and beliefs about the "efficiency" of Congress as a political institution, the ease with which a change in society is reflected in a change in the personnel and policies of Congress, how much congressional decisions are influenced by political party considerations, whether Congress has full discussion and debate of public issues, whether congressmen are among the more intelligent and capable men in the society, the manner in which congressmen make their decisions—that is, whether in terms of the "national interest" or in terms of their private interests or the interests of the particular groups of people who elected them—may also affect one's attitude toward Congress as an institution. Hence the phrase "other things being equal" may be dropped when a *series* of arguments (interrelated values and beliefs) are considered. When only one argument is being considered, as in the present case, "other things being equal" must be retained.[10]

We have said that attitudes have two components, affective (like and dislike) and cognitive (belief-disbelief). We have also shown that attitudes may be considered to be the conclusion to a series of (partial) syllogistic arguments containing values and beliefs as premises. The affective component of attitudes (measured in terms of direction and intensity) is reflected in the content and intensity of the values involved, and the cognitive component of attitudes are the beliefs involved. But there is another distinction regarding beliefs which it will be useful to make here.

Earlier in this chapter we referred to the notion that some beliefs are more "fuzzy" than others. By this we mean that beliefs may be differentiated on the basis of how "concretely" they refer to the real world. For example, the belief that "Johnny Jones has brown hair" is more easily *verified* than the belief that "Johnny Jones is honest." With the latter belief we have real problems determining what is meant by "honest." Different people may define honesty in different ways. On the other hand, we are less likely to have problems in defining "brown hair."

Putting this in a political context, we find that some people are more likely than others to express their political beliefs in terms of "honesty," "corruption," "Communism in government," "war," "depression," "religion," and other concepts which are rather difficult to define. Others are more likely to express their political beliefs in terms of more "concrete" issues, such as "level of tariffs," "level of farm price supports," "union shop vs. closed shop," which are a little more easily defined. Bernard Berelson makes a similar distinction between "style" and "position" issues.[11]

As we shall be using the terms, *style* issues are those issues concerning moral and ethical questions which tend, in our terminology, to be "fuzzy" and difficult to pin down to a particular meaning. For example, we may all be in favor of "peace," but under what conditions?

---

[10] See Lewis A. Froman, Jr., *Cognitive Consistency of Political Values and Beliefs* (unpublished Ph.D. dissertation, Northwestern University, Evanston, Illinois, 1960).

[11] Bernard Berelson, Paul F. Lazarsfeld, and William N. McPhee, *Voting* (Chicago: University of Chicago Press, 1954), p. 184.

Peace may be had at the price of submission to the enemy or, perhaps, by forcefully attempting to impose your conditions on others, or any of the many states of affairs in between these two extremes. In other words, "peace," like "democracy," "liberty," "justice," and so forth, may mean different things to different people. Such concepts are at a high level of abstraction. They may signify a great number of different situations.

Position issues, on the other hand, have a more concrete meaning. They are, in this sense, closer to reality and more easily translated into measurable units of analysis. For example, by an "adequate level of farm price supports" some people mean ninety per cent of parity. Others may mean seventy-five per cent of parity. The difference is measurable and meaningful in concrete terms. Disputes tend to occur among people over how much parity, not over what it means.

A word of caution is now in order. Any attempt to divide political issues into two and only two kinds will tend to simplify and perhaps distort the real world. That is, some issues may not neatly fit into one and only one category. Take a civil rights issue, for example. This would fall under our category of a style issue. Civil rights issues tend to be cast in moral and ethical terms (for example, "All men are created equal," or "We should not have any 'second-class' citizens"). But specific and concrete proposals are often involved in style issues, for example, whether a civil rights commission should be established in the Department of Justice to help Negroes achieve voting rights. Basically, however, such issues are cast in broad, general, and vague terms ("humanitarianism" versus "states rights") and hence can be considered predominantly style issues. Although, then, there will be some overlap on issues—that is, some issues will have elements of both style and position types—we should be able to make useful distinctions depending upon which elements tend to predominate. We can also view the distinction between style and position issues as a continuum from highly abstract to highly concrete. Some issues may fall near the center of this continuum.

This distinction between style and position issues has a number of important consequences for politics, which will be discussed at some length in later chapters. For example, because style issues are broad and vague and are concerned with social and political principles, they tend to have wide appeal with the electorate at large. They are the kind of issues in which most people are interested (if they are interested in issues at all). Hence, they are perfectly suited for politicians who are trying to win mass support for one reason or another, and many politicians engage in the process of redefining essentially position issues, such as, for example, the level of taxes on corporations, into style issues, for example, government intervention in the economy. But more of this later.

One important consequence of this distinction between style and position issues that merits immediate attention is that style and position issues tend to have different effects upon the distribution of advantages and disadvantages. Style issues are primarily useful in the distribution of *symbolic* rewards and punishments. By "symbolic" I mean advantages and disadvantages that have little immediate impact on the lives of people. Position issues, on the other hand, are primarily useful in the distribution of *material* rewards and punishments. By "material" I mean advantages and disadvantages that tend to have relatively large, immediate consequences on the lives of a number of people.[12] Let me illustrate by example. Some public policies have an immediate and far-reaching effect on people. Legislation appropriating funds to help build two million new housing units in two years is a "reward" which is both immediate and large in its impact on citizens. The benefits of such legislation are relatively widespread and immediately felt. So, too, are the costs of federally subsidized housing felt among a rather large number of people. Legislation, however, that authorizes the Department of Justice to bring charges against corporations acting in "restraint of trade" may or may not have an immediate and large impact, depending upon how it is interpreted and enforced. Although on the surface such a piece of public policy may seem as though it *should* have wide and immediate impact, its execution (or lack thereof) may give it only symbolic significance.[13]

Style issues, then, are primarily involved in the distribution of symbolic and position issues in the distribution of material advantages and disadvantages. These relationships have enormous practical consequences for the politics involved in the distribution of such advantages and disadvantages in the population. Some people are more likely

---

[12] I am indebted to Professors Jack W. Peltason and Murray Edelman for helping me to clarify the distinction between symbolic and material advantages and disadvantages.

[13] See Murray Edelman, "Symbols and Political Quiescence," *American Political Science Review,* vol. 54 (September, 1960), pp. 695–705.

to emphasize, know about, talk about, and decide upon the basis of style rather than position issues. In fact, public opinion polls show that knowledge or information about position issues is extremely limited among the general population, and that most people make political choices on the basis of party identification (itself an attitude often based on "fuzzy beliefs") and the personality of the candidate (an example of a style issue).[14] We shall return to a more detailed discussion of the political consequences of these findings in later chapters.

We are now in a position to summarize, in propositional form, some of the salient features of our value-belief-attitude theory.[15] These propositions will be discussed at some length in the chapter to follow and are listed here only by way of introduction.

1. The greater the number of values related to an attitude, the greater the number of beliefs about the attitude object.
2. The more intense the values related to an attitude, the greater the number of beliefs about the attitude object.
3. The greater the number of beliefs about the attitude object, the more intense the attitude.
4. The greater the number of values related to an attitude, the more intense the attitude (deducible from 1 and 3).
5. The more intense the values related to an attitude, the more intense the attitude (deducible from 2 and 3).
6. The more intense an attitude, the more resistant it is to change.[16]
7. The greater the number of beliefs about the attitude object, the more resistant the attitude is to change (deducible from 3 and 6).

---

14 See Herbert H. Hyman and Paul B. Sheatsley, "The Current Status of American Public Opinion," in Daniel Katz, Dorwin Cartwright, Samuel Eldersveld, and Alfred McClung Lee, eds., *Public Opinion and Propaganda* (New York: Holt, Rinehart, and Winston, 1954), pp. 33–49; Paul F. Lazarsfeld, Bernard Berelson, and Hazel Gaudet, *The People's Choice*, 2nd ed. (New York: Columbia University Press, 1948); Bernard Berelson, *et al.*, *Voting*; Angus Campbell, Gerald Gurin, and Warren E. Miller, *The Voter Decides* (Evanston: Row, Peterson and Co., 1954); and Angus Campbell, Philip Converse, Warren E. Miller, and Donald Stokes, *The American Voter* (New York: John Wiley & Sons, Inc., 1960).

15 Propositions 1 through 13 were first proposed in Lewis A. Froman, Jr., "Learning Political Attitudes," *Western Political Quarterly*, vol. 15 (June, 1962).

16 Intensity of attitudes can be measured independently from resistance to change. For a discussion of measurement problems and a description of how these problems were handled in a research situation, see Lewis A. Froman, Jr., *Cognitive Consistency. . . .*

8. The greater the number of values related to an attitude, the more resistant the attitude is to change (deducible from 4 and 6).
9. The more intense the values related to an attitude, the more resistant the attitude is to change (deducible from 5 and 6).
10. The more intense an attitude, the more likely is it that the attitude will manifest itself in overt behavior.
11. The greater the number of beliefs about the attitude object, the more likely it is that the attitude will manifest itself in overt behavior (deducible from 3 and 10).
12. The greater the number of values related to an attitude, the more likely it is that the attitude will manifest itself in overt behavior (deducible from 4 and 10).
13. The more intense the values related to an attitude, the more likely it is that the attitude will manifest itself in overt behavior (deducible from 5 and 10).
14. The less issue-oriented the voter, the more his concern is with style issues rather than position issues.
15. The more a person's concern with style issues, the more likely he is to be satisfied with symbolic rewards.
16. The less issue-oriented the voter, the more likely he is to be satisfied with symbolic rewards (deducible from 14 and 15).

These hypotheses, which have a multitude of consequences for political behavior, will be explored in the next chapters. But basically, people in certain kinds of political relationships with others are more likely to be intense in their attitudes, have a greater number of beliefs, and so forth. An understanding of these factors aids considerably in explaining how our political system works.

Learning Values, Beliefs, and Attitudes

The learning of politically relevant values, beliefs, and attitudes begins at a relatively early age. There is evidence, for example, that by the fourth grade, school children have already learned certain "images" of the President and other political figures and have learned to respond with positive affection toward them. As the child increases in age, however, his highly positive image of political figures decreases until, by the age of sixteen or so, his attitudes and beliefs toward politics and political questions resemble quite closely those of adults.[17]

---

[17] See Robert D. Hess and David Easton, "The Child's Changing Image of the President," *Public Opinion Quarterly*, vol. 24 (Winter, 1960),

One researcher finds that American college students have already developed their "basic" value orientations before they come to college and that the experience of four years of college does little, if anything, to modify these values.[18] This conclusion, however, is disputed by many. Whether college students are likely to change in their political orientations and interests seems to depend upon the general political orientation on campus, their previous political experiences, and other factors that may produce a social environment highly conducive to change.[19]

Children learn their political values, beliefs, and attitudes from a variety of sources, including parents, friends, schoolteachers, and the mass media, but by far the most important influence comes from the family. There is considerable evidence, for example, that first-voters cast their ballots in seventy-five per cent of the cases for the same political party as that of their parents.[20] This rather high correlation between parents' vote and child's vote is evidence that the family is quite influential in directing the child into his political choices. It is also indirect evidence that party identification is one of the most important variables in explaining political choices.

But the study of political socialization is not reserved exclusively for children. Adults, too, are constantly learning from their friends, relatives, co-workers, and others in their social environment. Wives, for example, will almost always follow the political lead of their husbands.[21] Another researcher finds that, even among adults, stability

---

pp. 632–644; Fred I. Greenstein, "The Benevolent Leader: Children's Image of Political Authority," *American Political Science Review*, vol. 54 (December, 1960), pp. 934–944; and Herbert Hyman, *Political Socialization* (New York: Free Press of Glencoe, 1959).

18 Phillip E. Jacob, *Changing Values in College* (New York: Harper & Brothers, 1957), p. 55.

19 A. H. Barton, *Studying the Effects of College Education: A Methodological Examination of "Changing Values in College"* (New Haven: The Edward W. Hazen Foundation, 1959); and Theodore M. Newcomb, *Personality and Social Change* (New York: Holt, Rinehart, and Winston, 1943).

20 See Lazarsfeld, *et al.*, *The People's Choice*, p. 142; Berelson, *et al.*, *Voting*, p. 89; Campbell, *et al.*, *The Voter Decides*, pp. 97–107; Campbell, *et al.*, *The American Voter*, p. 147; E. Havemann and P. West, *They Went to College* (New York: Harcourt, Brace and Company, 1952), p. 117; and Hyman, *Political Socialization*, Chap. 4, for a review of the literature relating to parental party identification and party identification of children.

21 Lazarsfeld, *et al.*, *The People's Choice*, p. 142.

of party preferences is related to many environmental factors provided by the family. For example, the more homogeneous the party preferences of family members and the more intense their interest in politics and their loyalty to their party, the more stable is an individual's party preference.[22]

We can say, then, that a person's social environment provides many cues that help to structure his political behavior. Where the individual's environment is homogeneous in political outlook, his party preferences and voting patterns will be relatively stable. Where, on the other hand, his social environment consists of persons with differing political attitudes, he is less likely to talk about politics or to engage in political activity such as voting. The conflict in the environment is mirrored within himself and he tends, as a result, to withdraw from politics.

---

[22] Herbert McClosky and Harold E. Dahlgren, "Primary Group Influence on Party Loyalty," *American Political Science Review*, vol. 53 (September, 1959), pp. 757–776.

3

GROUPS

AND POLITICS

The study of politics is more than looking at individuals acting alone. True, many important aspects of political life, such as voting, writing letters to congressmen, and keeping abreast of political events, are individual acts. But, as we saw in the last chapter, one of the most significant factors influencing individual behavior is the fact that man lives in a social environment and learns many of his ways of behaving from others.

We can view individuals as having many values, beliefs, and attitudes involving the world about them, many of which have direct relevance to how they behave politically. People are brought up in an ongoing political system. They learn from their parents, friends, schoolmates, business associates, and so forth, to value certain things— for example, the free-enterprise system, democracy, free speech. They learn common ways of responding to various stimuli from their environment (voting or not voting, or voting for Democrats rather than Republicans). And they learn various reasons why their actions are "good" or "bad." People come to develop attitudes about a great number of things in their environment in this way: attitudes toward police protection, national defense, welfare legislation, protection of business, the electoral process, and so forth.

These learned values, attitudes, and beliefs are likely to be similar among certain kinds of individuals but not among others. What is it that makes some individuals similar in their political behavior and others different? Why is it, for example, that some people are Democrats and others Republicans? One answer to this question is that the type of environment in which a person lives helps to determine the kind of attitudes he will have, and people share common environments with others. Similar environments will tend to result in similar attitudes and behavior—a fact that has been demonstrated time and time again.[1] For example, a person's race, religion, occupation, income, and social status put him into contact with others who are similarly situated. These people will often have common needs and meet with similar frustrations. Because of their similar life situations, they develop common preferences and attitudes regarding political events and persons.

These similar attitudes and preferences find expression in political behavior. Generally speaking, men, younger voters, Catholics, Jews, Negroes, other minority groups, those in metropolitan centers, non-college-educated, skilled and unskilled blue-collar workers, union members, and low-income groups support the Democrats, while (again, generally speaking) women, older voters, Protestants, Whites, those in suburban and rural areas, college-educated, professional, business or managerial, sales, non-union, and high-income groups support the Republicans.[2] This is not to say that there are not exceptions to the above generalizations—there are many. It is merely to say that the groups mentioned are *more likely* than non-group members to support one party over the other. Nor is it to say that all environmental influences have similar effects. For example, although men tend to support the Democrats more than do women, the difference is not

---

[1] The voting-behavior literature is replete with data confirming this proposition. See especially Paul F. Lazarsfeld, Bernard Berelson, and Hazel Gaudet, *The People's Choice*, 2nd ed. (New York: Columbia University Press, 1948); Bernard Berelson, Paul F. Lazarsfeld, and William N. McPhee, *Voting* (Chicago: University of Chicago Press, 1954); and Angus Campbell, Philip E. Converse, Warren E. Miller, and Donald E. Stokes, *The American Voter* (New York: John Wiley & Son, Inc., 1960).

[2] See Seymour M. Lipset, Paul F. Lazarsfeld, Allen H. Barton, and Juan Linz, "The Psychology of Voting: An Analysis of Political Behavior," in Gardner Lindzey, ed., *The Handbook of Social Psychology* (Reading, Mass.: Addison-Wesley Publishing Co., Inc., 1954), vol. 2, pp. 1124–1177.

as large as the difference between low- and high-income groups. Generally speaking, as groups narrow in size, the members' behavior tends to be more similar.

The connecting link, then, between an individual's political behavior and the behavior of people in groups is that, because of common environmental influences (of which membership in the group is only one, such things as social class, education, and occupation usually being homogeneous among group members), group members tend to have similar values, beliefs, and attitudes. For example, interest groups that send representatives to Washington for the purpose of letting government officials know of the group's views and preferences on governmental business affecting the group are composed of individuals with at least one common characteristic (and usually, of course, many more). Many of these groups are occupational in character, for example, the National Association of Retail Druggists, the United Automobile Workers, and the American Farm Bureau Federation. Some groups are race-oriented, for example, the National Association for the Advancement of Colored People, and various White Citizens' Councils in the South. Others have "good government" interests and are organized for the purpose of promoting voting turnout, knowledge of issues, and other educational and informational services, for example, the League of Women Voters. These groups, in various ways, attempt to promote the interests of their members, for example, higher wages and better working conditions, favorable interest rates, equal rights for all citizens regardless of race, participation in political activities, and so forth.

The interest of political scientists in the behavior of groups stems from two sources: (1) the internal processes of group decision-making, from which we can learn a great deal about "private" democracy; and (2) the external relationships of groups with one another and with government officials, from which we can learn about the workings of "public" democracy. For example, with respect to the latter, there are many advantages for people to organize into groups for the purpose of satisfying their demands.[3] Those who are in a position to

---

[3] Arthur F. Bentley, *The Process of Government* (Bloomington, Indiana: Principia Press, 1949 reissue); V. O. Key, Jr., *Politics, Parties, and Pressure Groups*, 4th ed. (New York: Thomas Y. Crowell Company, 1958); Earl Latham, *The Group Basis of Politics* (Ithaca: Cornell University Press, 1952); and David B. Truman, *The Governmental Process* (New York: Alfred A. Knopf, Inc., 1951).

influence the distribution of advantages and disadvantages (such as congressmen, administrative personnel, and judges) are, generally speaking, impressed by numbers. This is especially true if those upon whom pressure is brought to bear are elective officeholders. Hence, access to public officials is easier (and probably more effective) if a relatively large and organized group of people is involved (although, as we shall see, smaller groups have the advantage of being more cohesive).

Also, groups often have resources unavailable to single individuals: large amounts of money (often from dues and special assessments), prestige, a full-time leadership looking after the interests of the organization, a considerable amount of knowledge—both with respect to the issues involved and the "know-how" in getting things done—and many other resources that result from the pooling of individual contributions into a collective enterprise and that individuals would find it next to impossible to muster for themselves. The study of politics, then, is very much concerned with groups and the pressures they bring to bear upon government. We shall return to a more detailed discussion of the external relationships of groups in later chapters. In this chapter, however, we shall concentrate our attention almost entirely upon the internal processes of group decision-making and factors that distinguish group members from one another.

Differences Among Group Members

We all have noticed in the groups to which we belong that some members become leaders and others do not, that some members participate in group activities more than others do, and that some seem to be more interested than others in things that have to do with the expressed purpose of the group. This differential behavior on the part of group members results from three very significant facts about people:

1. Individuals have many interests, and the amount of time and resources at their disposal is limited. Individuals must, therefore, allocate their time and energy according to their own values if they are to achieve the multiple purposes that they set for themselves. Very seldom does one interest become so dominant that a person will devote all his time and resources to one activity.

2. Different individuals have different interests and different in-

tensities of feelings regarding those interests. All of us have a variety of interests in life, and some we feel more intensely about than others. For some of us, participation in group activities is low in our priority system; for others, it may be high. The variation can stem not only from differences among individuals as to how much they like to participate in group activities; it can also vary in individuals from group to group.

3. Individuals join groups for a wide variety of reasons, and not always is the expressed purpose of the group the primary reason for joining. Factors such as prestige in being a group member or in making business contacts, or liking the sociability related to group life, are also important.

Groups, then, are made up of people with heterogeneous interests and with varying intensities of interest in group goals. These considerations of the internal composition of groups have a number of important consequences that are related to external relations of the group. We can, even at this point in our discussion, make several important generalizations:

1. The larger the group, the more likely it is that it will be made up of people with different interests and with a wide range of intensity with respect to their interests; conversely, the smaller the group, the more likely it is that individuals will be more homogeneous in their interests.

2. Homogeneity of interests is one factor that leads to group cohesion: the more homogeneous the group, the more cohesive the group. Hence, deducing from propositions 1 and 2, the smaller the group, the more likely it is to be cohesive.

3. Cohesiveness of groups is a factor that helps to explain why some groups are more effective in politics than others: the more cohesive the group, the greater its political effectiveness.[4] Cohesive groups are likely to be more politically effective because they have a greater proportion of the group membership sharing in common group goals, and because the level of intensity of interest in group goals is likely to be high. Hence, participation in group enterprises is also likely to be high. Being more intense and more persistent, cohesive groups are able to "wear down" the opposition, to attack on a number of

---

[4] Truman, *The Governmental Process,* Chap. 6. See also Peter Odegard, *Pressure Politics: The Study of the Anti-Saloon League* (New York: Columbia University Press, 1928).

fronts, and to let government decision-makers know what their views are and the consequences for not taking action on them.

4. Hence, it is not always the case that large groups are more effective in politics than are small groups. Large groups have the advantage of numbers, but small groups are likely to have the advantage of cohesiveness.

5. Also, large groups find it more difficult than do small groups to take positions on issues that will be satisfactory to all the members. Their stands on issues must necessarily be broad, general, and vague. This means, of course, that it is more difficult for governmental decision-makers to know just what the group wants and how intensely it wants it. In order to avoid schisms in the group, larger groups must sacrifice clarity of group preferences and, concomitantly, some of their political effectiveness. We shall have more to say about this in the final chapter.

Heterogeneity of interests and differences in intensity of interest in group goals tend to separate group members into three types: leaders, interested followers, and uninterested followers. This division is also helpful in setting the stage for a discussion of the internal politics of groups. For the moment, let us distinguish among the three types of group members.

1. *Leaders.* In all groups there are those who take a major interest in the group's activities and who get into positions that permit them to affect the interests of the whole group. Leaders may have a variety of motives for wanting to be in a position to influence the outcome of the group's decisions. For example, leaders may tend to have certain kinds of personalities which, when combined with the situational opportunities leading to positions of leadership (such as being close friends with past leaders, since leadership recruitment in groups often tends to be by co-optation), tend to distinguish leaders from non-leaders. For example, leaders may prefer being in a position of power in which they may manipulate others, dominate group proceedings, influence decisions, and so forth. The literature on personality differences among leaders and followers, however, is quite in doubt on this point, and probably not too much weight should be placed on it as an explanation of why some people become leaders and others do not.[5]

---

[5] See Robert E. Lane, *Political Life* (New York: Free Press of Glencoe, 1959) ; Alvin W. Gouldner, "Approaches to Leadership," in S. Sidney

About all that can be said at present is that leaders tend to possess certain skills that make them stand out in group activities. These skills, of course, tend to vary from group to group. Situational variables seem to be at least as important as personality factors in the recruitment of leaders.

Another motive for wanting to be a leader centers around the material advantages that are available to people in such positions. There is no doubt that very often in groups there are many material advantages in being in the group leadership that do not accrue to the regular membership. This is especially true of lower-class groups (for example, labor unions).[6] Leaders are usually considerably better paid than are the group members, and they have much more job security. Group leadership in voluntary and semi-voluntary organizations tends to be highly stable. This is the result of such factors as apathy on the part of the membership, monopoly of information and manipulative skills on the part of the leadership, control over means of communication, control over the nomination process, and so forth. For many lower-class individuals, becoming a group leader is a source of prestige, a "moving-up" in the social status hierarchy. It means being able to join the white-collar work force and no longer having to earn a living through manual labor—all of which makes being a leader a much more comfortable position.[7] These material advantages can be viewed as valued items among group members, the natural result being that, once in a position of leadership, a group member tries not to lose his position. This leads to a variety of actions on the part of the leadership that are designed to keep them firmly entrenched in office (a point that will be discussed in more detail later on).

A third factor that tends to result in some group members being leaders and others not is how intense members feel about group values. Aside from the material advantages involved in group leadership, it is also possible that the leaders of any group are those who feel very strongly about the interests that the group is trying to promote. In fact, it is likely that this is one factor influencing the

Ulmer, ed., *Introductory Readings in Political Behavior* (Chicago: Rand, McNally & Co., 1961), pp. 447–458; and Dorwin Cartwright and Alvin Zander, *Group Dynamics* (Evanston: Row, Peterson and Co., 1960), 2nd ed., Part 5.

6 Seymour M. Lipset, Martin Trow, and James Coleman, *Union Democracy* (New York: Free Press of Glencoe, 1956).

7 Lipset, Trow, and Coleman, *Union Democracy*, Chap. 1.

way in which leadership is originally recruited. Once in a position of leadership, however, the leader will want to remain in office for the reasons just given. To paraphrase a very significant finding by Lipset, Trow, and Coleman: [8] the greater the difference in status between followers and leaders, the more the leaders will want to stay in office for personal gain. It is undoubtedly the case, however, that leaders share certain important values with the membership, that they are intense about those values, and that they will attempt to carry out actions leading to the satisfaction of those values if for no other reason than to remain in office.

2. Interested followers. Returning to a second type of group member, we can distinguish those who take an active interest in group activities, go to meetings, contribute money, and so forth, but are not officers of the group. It is often from this category of members that leaders are recruited.

3. Uninterested followers. A third category of group members are those who merely belong to a group because they have to (non-voluntary or semi-voluntary group) or because they only weakly identify with the group's goals. They are also the people who see very little chance or have very little desire to become leaders of the group.

Leaders and Followers

In the previous sections, we have suggested that behavior can be at least partially explained in terms of the predispositions that people have learned over the years. We have also suggested that common experiences lead to similar predispositions, and that group members are likely to have common backgrounds and hence similar values, attitudes, and beliefs. But this does not mean that group members will be completely homogeneous in outlook and behavior; in fact, there are a variety of reasons why some people will become more active in groups than will others. Group homogeneity depends, among other things, upon the size of the group, the reasons for joining, and the intensity in group goals.

We are now in a position to take up two very important questions: (1) in what ways do leaders and non-leaders differ? and (2) what

---

[8] Lipset, Trow, and Coleman, *Union Democracy,* pp. 10–11.

important political consequences do these differences have? For our purpose, we shall speak only of leaders and followers (or non-leaders) rather than divide the followers into interested and uninterested. It should be kept firmly in mind, however, that some followers are less active than others, and possess even less of the characteristics than we shall indicate of followers in general as opposed to those of leaders in general.

One of the central notions of this book is that people differ in the nature of their predispositions to act, and that these differences have enormous consequences for how they act politically. Not only are there content differences with respect to people's predispositions— that is, different people are likely to have different preferences—but there are also differences in the intensity with which preferences are held. Following along this train of thought, then, one of the most important ways in which leaders and followers differ is in the nature of their values, attitudes, and beliefs. These differences, when made explicit, will help us to understand differences in the political behavior of people and will lay the foundation for a discussion of the politics of group life. In explicating these differences, we shall rely heavily on the propositions concerning people's predispositions given in Chapter 2.

With respect to the manner in which leaders and followers view the group of which they are a part, it is predicted that leaders will have the following characteristics:

1. Leaders have more values relating to why they are in the group. Group leaders gain a number of satisfactions from the group. Not only do they help to achieve group purposes (such as higher wages and better working conditions for group members), they also gain material satisfaction from their own position in the group. Theirs is a double role: satisfaction of organizational goals (in some instances, their position of leadership depends upon membership satisfaction with the way in which these goals are being achieved) and the satisfaction of their own material interests. This is, after all, their job; and, like most people, they wish to retain their job, at least until something better comes along. And, of course, there may be an added incentive to retain a leadership position: not to do so may mean going back to a less prestigious, poorer-paying job.

This dual nature of leadership values affects rather critically the attitudes of leaders toward the group. Their position in the group is seen as more than an attempt to achieve the avowed purpose of the group; it is also a means by which leaders may satisfy their own desires for esteem, wealth, and so forth. This is one of the most important factors in leader-follower relationships, and has a number of consequences relating to the group's success in politics, a point to which we shall return shortly.

2. Leaders are more intense about their values. Leaders are in a position in the group to make decisions that can have important consequences not only for the members of their group, but for themselves as well. At times, it is quite possible that what the leaders decide to do may have implications for their very position in the group. Since this is the case, their values regarding the group and their own position in it are held much more intensely than are the values of non-leaders. Leaders are much more group-oriented; that is, the group is much more important to them in their value system.

Leaders also have contact with other leaders outside the group who are in a position to oppose the interests of the group in question. This tends to sharpen the lines of dispute and to make the values that are in the controversy much more salient to leaders.[9]

3. Leaders have more beliefs concerning the group and the group's relations with other groups, the government, issues affecting the group, and so forth. Leaders, because of their position in the group and their constant contact with others outside the group concerning issues and policies affecting group interests, are more knowledgeable not only about issues affecting the group, but about the opinions and desires of group members. Leaders have opinions about more things, and they are better able to assimilate new information—accept it, reject it, or modify it—according to their own predispositions. Their current knowledge helps them to put into perspective other knowledge that they receive. They are also purveyors of information, not only with respect to their own membership but also with respect to those with whom they come into contact outside of the group.

After a short period, leaders may develop a rather elaborate belief system or ideology with regard to why the group wants certain things. This ideology develops into a justification for taking certain actions, both with other groups and with the membership of the group itself.

---

[9] Herbert McClosky, Paul J. Hoffman, and Rosemary O'Hara, "Issue Conflict and Consensus Among Party Leaders and Followers," *American Political Science Review*, vol. 54 (June, 1960), pp. 406–428.

The ideology may be used for propaganda purposes to manipulate others. Also, an ideology may be a basis upon which leaders make decisions as well as justify them. Ideologies provide leaders with a set of beliefs that help them to orient themselves to a rather complex world. Ideologies may, then, on occasion be viewed as "motives" as well as "rationalizations." [10]

4. Leaders are more intense than non-leaders in their attitudes. As a consequence of their greater number of values and beliefs, and their greater intensity of values regarding the group and its relations with others, group leaders are more intense in their attitudes about things that affect the group. Their attitude structure is one that is related to a wide range of values (material and group-centered), a relatively intense set of values, and a relatively large number of beliefs. Their attitudes regarding things that affect the group thereby take on the significance and firmness of persons in positions of potential power who have made up their minds, who have thought about issues, who have assimilated information relevant to their values, and who have learned to evaluate occurrences with respect to the importance of the event to themselves and to the group.

This intensity in attitudes, of course, is functional in many respects for the group leaders. They have the appearance of "knowing what's up," of how to handle events, and, especially, how to evaluate them. They are thus able to pass on to the group members information and evaluations regarding events within and outside of the group. They are able to hold the group's attention and influence the attitudes of the group members regarding these events. They are, in this sense, able to "lead" the group.

5. Leaders' attitudes are more resistant to change. Because of their intensity of values, and the greater number of their values and beliefs about the group and the world outside the group, leaders are much more resistant to change with respect to their evaluations of the forces impinging upon the group. This stability of attitudes has a number of important consequences for the way the political system functions. For example, leaders are more likely than non-leaders to be hard bargainers. They are less likely to be "pushed around" or persuaded of the "correctness" of someone else's position in the bargaining process. They are also likely to have more "realistic" attitudes because

---

10 I want to thank Professor Ralph Goldman for bringing this point to my attention.

of their greater knowledge—a factor that also lends stability to their attitudes. They are much better able than non-leaders, because their attitudes are intense and hence resistant to change, to get what they want, both for themselves and for their followers.

Group leaders also provide an element of stability to the political process as a whole. Being more resistant to change, they stand in contrast to those who are easily swayed by personal and emotional appeals. Leaders are much more likely to influence the predispositions of non-leaders than for the reverse to occur.

6. Leaders are more likely to act on the basis of their attitudes. Intense attitudes, besides providing stability to a person's behavior, also are an indication that the values underlying the attitudes are intense. Leaders have more values, more intense values, and hence more intense attitudes. Those with intense attitudes are more likely to participate in activities that lead to the satisfaction of the values that lie behind the attitude intensity. Since the intense attitudes are related to intense values, leaders are likely to act in ways suggested by their attitudes.

Intense attitudes are also functional for the leader in that they provide him with a means of making decisions economically. Leaders are placed in a position in which they, by necessity, make decisions. Since intensity of attitudes leads to persistence in behavior, this means that leaders, because they face many situations requiring similar responses, are able to respond to routine problems without having to expend a great deal of time and energy. They are able to save themselves the time and energy needed to spend on "important" decisions.

7. Leaders are more issue-oriented. Because of their position in the group, leaders are more concerned with issues that affect the interests of the group than are non-leaders. Leaders come into contact daily with others who are engaged in the political process for the purpose of gaining advantages. Hence, issues are more salient for leaders—this is their stock in trade, the very thing about which their job is concerned. They must keep abreast of political events and issues and constantly inform themselves of occurrences that may affect the interests of the group they represent.

Two things follow from this greater issue-orientation of leaders (see propositions 14 and 15 in Chapter 2):

8. Leaders are more concerned with position issues than are non-leaders, and,

9. Leaders are more interested in material satisfactions than are non-leaders. Since leaders are engaged in gaining benefits for their members, and since they come up against others who are also so engaged, it becomes their task to get the best deal they can for their members. This requires that they not be sidetracked by issues that have nothing to do with the material well-being of their members. We shall return to this point at the end of this chapter.

10. Leaders tend to differentiate themselves from non-leaders and leaders of other groups more than do non-leaders.[11] Leaders find it necessary, in the bargaining process, to make their position distinct from the positions of others. This is both a result of their greater knowledge of issues and effects that issues have on the group, and of their role in the political process as bargaining agents for their members. They, by the very nature of bargaining, must see their position as different from those of others in order to gain leverage and to have something to "trade." They are then in a better position to offer compromises to others in the bargaining relationship. It is their job to get as much as they can for their group and for themselves. This requires that they make their own position as clear as possible and distinguish it from the positions of those around them.

Non-leaders, as has been implied throughout this analysis, are quite different from leaders on all ten of these characteristics. This follows, of course, from the position of followers vis-à-vis leaders. Non-leaders do not have as much at stake in the group, they seldom get agitated about anything that comes before the group, and they are inclined to be non-participators. In order to explain these findings, we suggest the following hypotheses:

1. Non-leaders have fewer values relating to why they are in the group. Followers, not being in the position of leadership that brings in its train values about staying in such a position, and not being in the position of having to consider, very often, group goals, have fewer values relating themselves to the group. As a consequence, group concerns are less important for non-leaders—there is less in group life that relates to values salient to them, and hence they are less interested.

2. Non-leaders are less intense about their values. Followers are much less likely to see the group as providing them with satisfactions to important values. They are, on the whole, concerned with other

---

[11] Herbert McClosky, *et al.,* "Issue Conflict . . .," pp. 425–427.

matters and, not having a great deal of knowledge about group activities, are much less likely to see the group as salient for the achievement of the values they do have. Decisions affecting the group do not take on the importance attached to them by leaders, who are immersed in group activity and who are much more perceptive of events and information affecting them.

3. Non-leaders have fewer beliefs concerning the group and the group's relations with other groups, the government, issues affecting the group, and so forth. Followers are less knowledgeable about group affairs and issues that affect the group. Because of their lower interest, followers are also less inclined to engage in activities (reading, talking, attending meetings) that will make them more knowledgeable.

4. Non-leaders are less intense in their attitudes. Given the fewer values, less intense values, and fewer beliefs of non-leaders, their attitudes about things that affect the group are at a relatively low temperature. They, in effect, find it difficult to understand "what's going on" and to do their own evaluating of events impinging upon the group. Hence, they are likely to take their cues in these matters from the leadership and, to fill the void in their own evaluations, to take over whatever the leadership is inclined to tell them.

This, of course, is quite functional for the leadership, as it gives them the opportunity to structure events as they themselves want to and in such a way that it most benefits them. It affords them the opportunity to manipulate opinion among group members. This, obviously, is a powerful tool in allowing the leadership to do what it wants to do and still act within an aura of legitimacy and group support.

5. Non-leaders' attitudes are less resistant to change. Because their attitudes are weak, based on few beliefs, and geared to few and weak values, followers are more open to persuasion, more likely to be moved in their attitudes both by outside influences and by their own leadership, and less likely to retain their attitudes in the face of strong pressures to the contrary. Hence, they are much more flexible in their attitudes than are leaders. But they are also much more likely to be swayed by propaganda.

This does not mean that non-leaders are completely open-minded about issues affecting the group.[12] They, like most people, do have

---

[12] I wish to thank Professor Ralph Goldman for suggesting many of the thoughts in this paragraph.

rigid attitudes (or prejudices) about a number of things: for example, who should be allowed to be a member of the group. Stouffer finds, for example, that community leaders tend to be less prejudiced than non-leaders toward many non-conformist groups.[13] These kinds of attitudes are likely to be fulfilling some inner need for the individual (see Chapter 2, ego-defensive attitudes). As these prejudices impinge upon group activities, non-leaders, too, can be inflexible. It is one of the tasks of leadership to insure that such inflexibility resulting from prejudice is put to use for the leadership and not against it.

However, we are speaking here primarily of utilitarian and knowledge attitudes. Leaders, because of their more comprehensive and intense value-belief-attitude structure, and because of their greater interest in group activities, are more likely than non-leaders to "have their minds made up" about issues affecting the group.

6. Non-leaders are less likely to act on the basis of their attitudes. Since non-leaders' attitudes are of relatively low intensity, based on little information and not connected with strong values, they are not likely to be moved to action by events affecting the group. For one thing, since they are limited in their knowledge about such events, they are less likely to see the connection or relevance of happenings outside the group to the group itself. Also, they lack the motivation (value system) which is likely to induce action to satisfy and reduce tensions brought to bear by outside occurrences. As a consequence, non-leaders are notoriously poor participators in group life. They do not attend many meetings, pay much attention to the nomination and election of leaders, or act in the group's behalf, and so forth. This, obviously, has enormously important consequences for the decision-making within the group.

7. Non-leaders are less issue-oriented. Followers, because of the factors mentioned above, do not pay very close attention to issues affecting the group. Their interests lie elsewhere, and usually only a cursory glance at the front page of a newspaper or listening to the news on radio or television serves as their contact with issues.

From this low issue-orientation on the part of non-leaders it follows that (see propositions 14 and 15 in Chapter 2):

8. Non-leaders are more interested in style issues than are leaders, and,

---

13 Samuel A. Stouffer, *Communism, Conformity, and Civil Liberties* (New York: Doubleday & Co., Inc., 1955), Chap. 2.

9. Non-leaders are more likely than leaders to be satisfied by symbolic advantages. The events that catch the attention of non-leaders are usually concerned with moral and emotion-laden issues. These kinds of events produce tensions that often have little to do with the material distribution of advantages and disadvantages. Leaders, of course, realize this and often try to "puff-up" their accomplishments and arouse the support of non-leaders by casting issues in style form. Hence, these tensions produced by style issues tend to be reduced by symbolic satisfactions and emotional gratifications.

10. Non-leaders tend, more than leaders, to see themselves as being like other people, regardless of whether others are fellow group-members or not. Followers are less likely to see people's stands on issues as being different from their own—especially the stand of those whom they like.[14] Non-leaders are less aware of issues, consider them less important, and are less interested in them. Nor are they in a position where it is important for them to differentiate themselves from non-group members. Hence, unlike leaders, they are less likely to see distinctions between themselves and others on issues.

These differences between leaders and non-leaders have two important political consequences regarding the internal decision-making of groups. The first we have already briefly discussed (propositions 7, 8, and 9 for both leaders and non-leaders). Because of a wider range of values, more intense values and attitudes, more beliefs, and more knowledge about events affecting the group, leaders are more issue-oriented than are non-leaders and are more likely to see the relevance of both group and outside activities for themselves and for group members. This higher degree of issue-orientation among leaders makes leaders both perceptive of and concerned with a wide range of concrete and specific proposals, that is, position issues. Leaders, of course, are also interested in position issues because, in no small measure, their own power and prestige are determined by their ability to win advantages for the group. The prestige that goes with the office, and the esteem that they themselves can garner for the manner in which they conduct themselves as leaders, are assets that they are not likely to relinquish voluntarily.

For these reasons leaders are far more concerned with immediate and noticeable benefits and are far less satisfied with symbolic assur-

---

14 Bernard Berelson, *et al., Voting,* Chap. 10.

ances that the interests of their group are being taken care of than are non-leaders. They much prefer to be able to bring to their groups specific, material gains. When they are unable to do so, they will either dress-up whatever gains they have achieved in symbolic form to reduce the tension created by group members' expectations of benefit and the actual benefit they received, or they may use their defeat as a style issue, characterizing the opposition as powerful and supported by selfish interests, in hopes of rallying their members for the next fight.

It follows, too, that influencing leaders will require strategies and tactics much different from those that may be employed in influencing followers. Leaders, since their attitudes are already quite intense and stable, cannot be easily swayed by emotional appeals. It is a much wiser strategy to work on a leader's belief structure, make him see connections he missed before, and illustrate how what he is getting is the best deal he can expect under the circumstances.

Followers, on the other hand, are more likely than are leaders to be satisfied with symbolic advantages. Followers have few beliefs connected with their attitudes about group life, their values are less numerous and less intense, and their attitudes are weaker. Also, they are less knowledgeable and less able to see the relevance of group activities to their own personal gain. They take less interest in group activities and participate less in them. The kinds of issues they are likely to get excited about are broad, general, moral questions—that is, style issues. To reduce these kinds of tensions, it is not necessary to provide material gains, but merely to promise that "things will improve," or that they have "right" on their side.

Hence, influencing followers involves appeals to emotion. Not being interested or knowledgeable about specific issues affecting the group, followers are more swayed by broad appeals for the attainment of some non-specific goal, such as "better" working conditions or "lower" interest rates.

A second important consequence stemming from the differences between leaders and non-leaders is what Michels has called "The Iron Law of Obligarchy." [15] Because people's interests are varied, and because different people have different value hierarchies—that is, consider different things as important to achieve—a division of labor in group activities ensues. Many take very little interest in group activities at

---

[15] Robert Michels, *Political Parties* (New York: Free Press of Glencoe, 1949).

all; others become group leaders and spend much of their time engaged in such activities. As a consequence, the leadership is put in the position of *having* to do most of the work for the group, whether they want to or not. This results in the group being dominated by a relatively few people who make most of the day-to-day decisions and who rely very little on the mass membership for guidance or direction. Leaders, of course, who carry on activities that can be attacked by an incipient opposition as not in the group's interest (corruption would be a good example) are courting defeat, but usually the members of the group can be counted on to approve leadership actions. Group members, because of their apathy regarding group activities, serve primarily a legitimatizing function for leaders, that is, they provide the means whereby the decisions of leaders are viewed as authoritative and legitimate because major decisions are brought to the group for its approval. The appearance of being "democratic" and having group support for decisions is obviously very important to leaders when bargaining with others.[16] It is therefore important for leaders to take into consideration the wishes of those who do attend meetings, and perhaps to attempt to insure victory by making certain that their partisans attend and vote.

The distinction, then, between leaders and non-leaders aids us considerably in explaining the internal politics of groups.

---

[16] Truman, *The Governmental Process*, p. 129.

4

TYPES OF POLITICAL

DECISION-MAKING

In Chapter 1 we suggested that the distribution of outcomes among any group of people is determined by: (1) the kind of people involved in the decision-making process and the resources they have to bring to bear on others; and (2) the type of decision-making process in which advantages are being distributed. In the last two chapters we have been primarily concerned with the first of these factors, that is, differences among people and how these differences are likely to affect who gets what in the political process. In this chapter we shall continue with the same distinctions, but we shall add a new dimension to our analysis. We shall be primarily concerned with exploring the types of interaction that occur among leaders and followers and the consequences that these systems of interaction have for the distribution of outcomes among people. Put another way, given our knowledge of people, what difference does the type of decision-making process make in the distribution of advantages and disadvantages?

To begin with, politics, with all its intricate maneuvering and its complex set of influence relationships, may be viewed as merely an elaboration of a primitive form of bartering. People occupy various positions in the social system, and accompanying these positions are various opportunities to influence the distribution of advantages and disadvantages. That is, different positions in society have attached to them different amounts of various kinds of resources, such as prestige, income, and time. For example, a construction laborer has, at the minimum, a vote. He may distribute this vote as he chooses among the alternatives presented to him by the political parties sponsoring candidates for office. He may also, however, have a little extra money to contribute to the party or candidate of his choice, or he may be willing to use some of his leisure time to stuff envelopes, ring doorbells, distribute literature, or engage in various other activities that he feels would help contribute to the success of his candidate or party.

A business executive, on the other hand, generally has more resources to insure the success of his candidate or party. Not only does he have a vote and perhaps time to solicit funds for the party of his choice, but he is also likely to have money, friends with money, a position of prestige in the community, access to politicians, and other resources that go along with his higher economic and social position.

There is one compensating factor, however, that tends to balance out the inequalities in individual positions in the social system. There are many more people with small resources than there are people with large resources. And since numbers are so important in a system in which candidates are elected by the number of votes they receive, when those with few individual resources band together, they are often able to outweigh those whose per capita resources are larger. For example, upper-income groups tend to support the Republican Party and lower-income groups the Democratic Party. At the present time, there are approximately three people who call themselves Democrats for every two who consider themselves Republicans. On the question of sheer number of supporters, the Democrats are far ahead.[1] (The lower turnout rate of Democrats as opposed to Republicans tends, however, to narrow this gap in numbers.)

Political resources, then, tend to be distributed unequally. But, as Robert Dahl cogently points out, inequalities in political resources tend to be dispersed, not cumulative. That is, those who have great wealth or prestige may not at the same time be popular or possess "legitimacy." Professor Dahl suggests the following as a list of political resources:

---

[1] See Angus Campbell, Philip E. Converse, Warren E. Miller, and Donald E. Stokes, *The American Voter* (New York: John Wiley & Sons, Inc., 1960), p. 124.

A list of resources in the American political system might include an individual's own time; access to money, credit, and wealth; control over jobs; control over information; esteem or social standing; the possession of charisma, popularity, legitimacy, legality; and the rights pertaining to public office. The list might also include solidarity: the capacity of a member of one segment of society to evoke support from others who identify him as like themselves because of similarities in occupation, social standing, religion, ethnic origin, or racial stock. The list would include the right to vote, intelligence, education, and perhaps even one's energy level.[2]

Professor Dahl then describes the characteristics of a system of dispersed inequalities.

This system of dispersed inequalities is, I believe, marked by the following six characteristics.

1. Many different kinds of resources for influencing officials are available to different citizens.

2. With few exceptions, these resources are unequally distributed.

3. Individuals best off in their access to one kind of resource are often badly off with respect to many other resources.

4. No one influence resource dominates all the others in all or even in most key decisions.

5. With some exceptions, an influence resource is effective in some issue-areas or in some specific decisions but not in all.

6. Virtually no one, and certainly no group of more than a few individuals, is entirely lacking in some influence resources.[3]

Hence, politics involves a lot of different people with a lot of different resources. The system is ripe for exchanges to take place. Each of the people occupying the various economic and social positions in society has certain wants and needs. These desires are often similar among people who are in similar positions.[4] Assuming a minimum amount of knowledge about how the game of politics is played, and given the fact that politicians are likely to court their support, people are able (at least in democratic political systems) to make their demands known. Often these demands will be made for

---

[2] Robert A. Dahl, *Who Governs? Democracy and Power in an American City* (New Haven: Yale University Press, 1961), p. 226. Reprinted by permission of Yale University Press.

[3] Robert A. Dahl, *Who Governs?*, p. 228. Reprinted by permission of Yale University Press.

[4] See the beginning of Chapter 3.

them by group leaders and political party representatives who have taken up their cause. These spokesmen may suggest to governmental decision-makers that they have certain advantages to give (votes, money, and so forth) in exchange for favors (for example, legislation that will meet the demands of those who are making the offer). This, in a most simplified version, is politics. We shall attempt, in this and the following chapters, to make this simplification more elegant and realistic. We shall begin by describing various forms of political decision-making and showing how the decision-making process influences the distribution of advantages and disadvantages.

If we continue to employ the distinction between leaders and followers made in the last chapter, we can, on the basis of this dichotomy, distinguish among four types of political systems, depending upon who is interacting with whom, and under what circumstances. The four systems of interaction are: (1) leaders interacting with leaders, (2) non-leaders interacting with non-leaders, (3) leaders interacting with non-leaders in a situation in which non-leaders elect leaders, and (4) leaders interacting with non-leaders in a situation in which non-leaders do not elect leaders. The first we shall call bargaining, the second discussion, the third democracy, and the fourth hierarchy.[5] Put in a fourfold table, the relationship would look something like this:

TABLE 1 FOUR POLITICAL SYSTEMS

	Leaders	Followers
Leaders	*Bargaining*—the resources of the participants are large	*Hierarchy*—leaders are not elected by non-leaders
Followers	*Democracy*—leaders are elected by non-leaders	*Discussion*—the resources of the participants are small

It will be noticed in Table 1 that we are differentiating among the four political systems along three demensions: leaders and fol-

---

[5] Robert A. Dahl, "Hierarchy, Democracy, and Bargaining in Politics and Economics," in Heinz Eulau, Samuel J. Eldersveld, and Morris Janowitz, eds., *Political Behavior* (New York: Free Press of Glencoe, 1956), pp. 83–90, has a slightly different treatment of similar relationships.

owers, the size of the resources which the participants bring to the interaction system (one of the factors differentiating bargaining from discussion), and whether or not the leaders are elected by non-leaders (distinguishing democracy from hierarchy). All three of these dimensions will be important to the following analysis.

Politics as Bargaining

Politics as bargaining is characterized by leaders interacting with leaders. This may take several forms:

1. Governmental officials interacting with each other:
   a. Within one branch of government, for example, members of Congress;
   b. Between branches of government, for example, the President with Congress.
2. Between government officials and leaders outside of government:
   a. With interest-group leaders;
   b. With other influentials, for example, political party officials.
3. Among non-governmental leaders, for example, bargaining among leaders of interest groups.

In each case the interactions involve people who are well-informed about the issue at hand, who have strong attitudes regarding the issue —attitudes that are highly resistant to change—who have a personal stake in the outcome (their ability to stay in office, as well as their prestige and esteem, may partially depend upon their success), who have a number of resources at their command, and who are interested in the material benefits involved in the issue. Their attitudes are mainly utilitarian (see Chapter 2): they have certain goals they wish to attain, and they are carrying on activities that they hope will allow them to achieve those goals. They are men who make politics their business and are not likely to be swayed by emotional appeals.

On any given issue, there will be leaders (both governmental and non-governmental) who are intensely interested in the outcome and are working for the success or defeat of the issue. Others will be only mildly interested in the outcome. Still others will be quite apathetic about the issue, either because it does not materially affect their specific interests or, in the case of governmental officials, the interests of a part of their constituency, or because they do not have intense values

regarding the issue. For example, since it takes a majority vote i
Congress to pass a particular piece of legislation (and the clearanc
by a number of Congressional leaders, including committee chairmen
those interested in passing the legislation must bargain with othe
(including the apathetic) to build a winning coalition. The politi
of bargaining in Congress is the politics of forming a majority coal
tion of leaders and insuring clearance through various committees b
bargaining with those leaders who are able to stall or prevent th
issue from coming to a vote.

Bargaining in politics, then, occurs under the following condi
tions:

1. A political decision is being made (that is, one which affects
   large number of people).
2. The preferred outcome of the decision is different for differen
   participants.
3. Those participating in the decision have a high degree of poten
   tial power, that is, they are leaders and directly engaged i
   influencing the decision (if they are interest-group leaders) o
   making the decision (if they are officeholders).
4. The participants in the decision have various intensities of desir
   regarding the outcome.

Bargaining involves offering others something in return for some
thing else. It costs more to change a person's mind than to move hin
from apathy to a position on an issue, and it costs more to chang
those who feel intensely about the issue than those who have onl
mild feelings. Hence, a person's ability to bargain depends in par
on what he has to offer (and what he is willing to offer) in return fo
something else, and in part on the willingness of others to bargair
in return. Bargaining also depends upon the structure of the situa
tion. That is, if the opposition are in positions of high potential powe
(for example, committee chairmen, the Speaker of the House), th
task will be made more difficult.

In attempting to gain something from someone else, one must be
prepared to give something in return. The fact that an exchange i
taking place, however, need not be made explicit between or among
the parties to a bargain. For example, when a congressman is approached by another leader (for example, the Speaker, a committee
chairman, the floor manager for a bill, another congressman, an administrative official, or an interest-group leader) to support a particular

ll, it is not necessary for the congressman to ask for a favor in return or to make explicit a *quid pro quo*. The congressman can count, however, on the other leader's "good will" for something that the congressman might want in the future. Both men know this, and nothing need be said about it. Many of the bargains in Congress are made in this implicit fashion. The parties understand that a bargain has been struck, and that the good will created will be negotiable sometime in the future.

Implicit bargaining is characteristic of formal organizations where interactions among members are relatively frequent. Implicit bargaining is not likely to take place among leaders who do not interact very often with each other. The reason is clear: to bargain implicitly, a leader wants some kind of guarantee that the favor will be returned. Formal organizations are likely to permit such guarantees because the personnel is relatively stable. This insures that at one time or another such bargains can be paid off. Also, norms about such guarantees may develop as members of the organization learn that, to get things done economically and for the benefit of all concerned, such implicit bargains are necessary.

There are two reasons why implicit bargaining is prevalent among those who are frequently in contact with one another. The first has to do with why implicit bargaining is necessary; the second with why it works successfully.

Implicit bargaining is necessary because leaders often do not know exactly what they want in exchange for a favor. Implicit bargaining usually involves some recognition that the leader asking for the favor is "indebted" to the other, but in a vague and ambiguous way. It is to the advantage of both parties to leave the matter ambiguous. For the leader asking the favor, it means that he need not commit himself early to a position that might later prove difficult to maintain because of other, more "important" pressures. For the leader granting the favor, it means that he, too, need not commit himself to a particular *quid pro quo*. He is then able to ask for a favor when he needs it most—something that he will not know until a matter of importance to him develops. Implicit bargaining, then, is necessary (where it is possible, that is, among leaders who interact frequently) because explicit bargaining is not feasible in many cases and involves costs (that is, committing early, which most politicians prefer not to do).

Second, implicit bargaining operates successfully among govern-

mental decision-makers because much of politics is coalition-buildin
If a leader wants something, he usually has to have at least a majori
of votes on his side. This is true for almost every issue. Because ba
gaining is necessary, and because implicit bargaining is often the rul
parties must honor their bargains. To "cheat" on bargains would plac
a leader in a difficult position. Without trust, implicit bargaining
impossible. Others will be reluctant to join in coalitions with an un
trustworthy bargainer. Since bargaining is so important in decisio
making, if a leader is interested in the outcome of a decision, he mu
be in a position to bargain. Hence he must not earn the reputatio
of one who does not pay off his political debts.

The two most common forms of bargaining are compromise an
logrolling. When a party to a bargain is asked to give in a little i
his demands in return for the other side giving in a little also, this
known as a *compromise*. Compromises usually involve explicit bar
gaining. That is, the nature of the negotiations is such that immediat
feedback is necessary. It is something like trading in a junk-shop. I
the price for an item is five dollars and you offer two dollars, to arriv
at a mutually satisfactory price usually involves several steps.

Compromises occur because leaders involved in decision-making ar
usually unable to agree immediately on a single course of action, espe
cially if the issue is significant by one or more of the criteria men
tioned in Chapter 1, for example, if the issue involves a large numbe
of people, or if it involves large outlays of money. Such issues affec
different leaders differently, depending in part on the interests the
represent. If a stalemate (which may be harmful to both sides) is t
be averted, each side must give in a little in its position. The resul
is something which probably does not please anyone perfectly but doe
represent a solution to which both sides can agree.

Logrolling occurs when a party to a bargain is asked to come int
a coalition with a person or persons on a particular issue in return
for support for the other person at some future time. This form o
bargaining represents a simple exchange of favors—support in return
for support. It differs from compromise in that no concession in a
person's original position is necessary. All that is required is a mutua
exchange of support on two different items. This is a prevalent form
of bargaining because not every item on an agenda interests every
leader to the same extent. For example, congressmen come from
different constituencies with different interests. To get a bill through
Congress requires a majority coalition, and such a coalition often

equires not only those with similar interests getting together but also aving the apathetic—that is, those with little or no interest in the neasure—join the coalition. Logrolling, then, is used as a method f building coalitions, and especially to gain support from the apathetic r only slightly interested.

Logrolling also differs from compromise in that bargains involving ogrolling are often implicit. Logrolling involves a mutual exchange f favors, and, as we have already seen, such a situation is best handled or both parties when the commitment is made vague and ambiguous. One need not know immediately what the payoff is or what asking for upport is going to cost. It is to the advantage of both if this is left ambiguous.

Some issues involve a "yes" or "no" answer. That is, they involve questions of initiating or terminating programs of one sort or another. These initiating and terminating questions tend to be dichotomous; hat is, they either are or are not initiated or terminated. Whether a civil rights commission is to be established in the Department of Justice, and whether foreign aid to Yugoslavia is to be terminated, are examples of dichotomous questions. Most issues, however, involve a matter of "how much." Rather than being strictly "yes" or "no," they involve questions of either increasing or decreasing by various amounts, or of keeping the level constant. How much authority a commission is to have, how much money is to be appropriated to allow it to carry out its functions, are examples of questions with a variety of solutions.

"Yes" or "no" issues are likely to involve participants in much more heated controversy than "how much" issues because compromise as a form of bargaining is often very difficult. On such questions attempts are sometimes made to change the question from one of "yes" or "no" to "how much," but it is often difficult to do so. Since the question is, for many of the participants, a proposition of "yes" or "no," there is no in-between course on which to settle. Hence, if stalemate is to be averted, some form of logrolling is necessary.

Proposals involving "how much," on the other hand, are much more susceptible to bargaining in the form of compromise. Both sides are able to reduce their demands to some extent, and a position in between the extremes may be found. Most appropriation bills in Congress are good examples of bargaining in which compromise is likely to be prevalent.

As we have already mentioned, whether a leader engages in compromise or logrolling is also a question of the extent of his commitmen on the issue. Those leaders who are apathetic are much more likel to join coalitions under logrolling arrangements. Those leaders wh have a definite commitment to one side or the other are much mor likely to find it necessary to compromise.

Bargaining as a form of distributing advantages and disadvantage is quite extensive in decision-making involving leaders. This situatior is due to the fact that leaders have different preferences, varying in tensities of desire, and varying amounts of different kinds of resources In order to satisfy their preferences, they must join coalitions witl others. This coalition-building involves both implicit and explici bargaining and varying amounts of compromise and logrolling, de- pending upon whether the leaders interact frequently, whether the issue is dichotomous or open to a variety of solutions, and whether or not leaders have made a commitment or have strong preferences regarding the issue.

Politics as Discussion

"Politics as discussion" is being used broadly here to mean any situation in which non-leaders find themselves discussing current events, the election, or any other topic having to do with politics. This kind of interaction situation provides the ordinary citizen the opportunity to do some reality-testing of his own ideas and preferences.

The first point that is of concern to us is that interest in politics among the mass public in the United States is low. Voting studies continually show that during election time—a period when interest in politics is highest—only about one-third of the adult population indicates that they are very much interested in the campaign, about one-third are moderately interested, and one-third are not interested at all.[6] Moreover, the uninterested are less likely to participate in political activities such as following the campaign in the mass media and, more importantly, voting.[7]

---

[6] Bernard Berelson, Paul F. Lazarsfeld, and William N. McPhee, *Voting* (Chicago: University of Chicago Press, 1954), p. 24; Angus Campbell, Gerald Gurin, and Warren E. Miller, *The Voter Decides* (Evanston: Row, Peterson and Company, 1954), p. 34; and Angus Campbell, *et al., The American Voter*, p. 103.

[7] Bernard Berelson, *et al., Voting*, p. 26; Angus Campbell, *et al., The Voter Decides*, p. 35; and Angus Campbell, *et al., The American Voter*, p. 103.

Not only is interest low, but information about political events is also low. Although information on how well-informed the public is on any given issue is nonexistent (Gallup Polls, for example, ask for the respondent's opinion, not information), several inferences can be made on the basis of data on issue-orientation of voters. Hyman and Sheatsley, from secondary analysis of a number of polls and surveys, report that ". . . between 60 and 70 per cent reported that they had no knowledge of what was in their party platforms during the 1948 presidential campaign, and when asked in the spring of that year to identify the position held by President Truman on six major issues, the average citizen could state only three of the six correctly; one person in five knew where Truman stood on only one or on none of them." [8]

Since interest in politics is low among the general population, and information about political issues and events is also low, we predict two things with respect to the discussion of politics in the mass public:

1. Few people will talk frequently about politics.
2. When people do talk about politics, they will stress opinions and evaluations rather than information.

With regard to the first proposition—that is, that few people will talk frequently about politics—after the election of Eisenhower in 1952, the Survey Research Center, which had been conducting a nationwide study during the campaign, asked their respondents to answer the question: "Did you talk to any people to try to show them why they should vote for one of the parties or candidates?" Only twenty-seven per cent of the total sample said "yes." [9] In a set of questions given to 8,000 adults designed to be representative of the country, Woodward and Roper found, in answer to their questions about political discussion, that twenty-one per cent of the sample reported discussing politics frequently and taking an equal share in the conversation, six per cent reported discussing frequently and attempting to convince others of the "rightness" of their position.[10] Berelson, *et al.*

---

8 Herbert H. Hyman and Paul B. Sheatsley, "The Current Status of American Public Opinion," in John C. Payne, ed., *The Teaching of Contemporary Affairs,* National Council for the Social Studies, 21st Yearbook, 1950, pp. 17–18. Reprinted by permission of The National Council for the Social Studies.

9 Angus Campbell, *et al., The Voter Decides,* p. 30.

10 Julian L. Woodward and Elmo Roper, "Political Activity of American Citizens," in Heinz Eulau, *et al.,* eds., *Political Behavior,* p. 135.

report, however, that many people can recall a political conversation with a member of their family, especially around election time: "Whereas only fifteen per cent of the discussants named another family member as the person with whom they had last discussed politics in June, this figure became fifty-two per cent in October, at the height of the campaign." [11] We can conclude that many people mention an upcoming election with at least a family member, but very few discuss politics with any frequency, and even fewer attempt to persuade others to change their minds.

With respect to the second proposition—that is, that when people do talk about politics, they will stress opinions and evaluations rather than information—we have no data that will test the proposition directly. However, we can make some inferences on the basis of the data we have:

    a. Like people will tend to talk politics to each other more often than unlike people.[12]

It has long been known that people tend to select from their environment those things that they like and approve, and to avoid things that they do not like. For example, with respect to the mass media, Democrats are more likely than Republicans to expose themselves to Democratic campaign activities, and Republicans are more likely than Democrats to expose themselves to Republican campaign activities.[13] This kind of harmonious interaction situation is conducive to the sharing of opinions and attitudes, and is not likely to lead to unbiased information exchange.

    b. Most people in the mass public have little political information. This, again, is indirect evidence that conversations among people tend to revolve around the mutual sharing of evaluations and opinions and not information exchange.

Conversations among non-leaders are likely to be liberally sprinkled with "shoulds" and "oughts," for example, "I think we should be tough with the Russians," or "I think the President is doing a lousy job." These are evaluative statements that provide no information

---

[11] Bernard Berelson, *et al.*, *Voting*, p. 102.

[12] Bernard Berelson, *et al.*, *Voting*, Chap. 6.

[13] For a review of the literature relating to self-selected exposure to media influences, see Joseph T. Klapper, *The Effects of Mass Communication* (New York: Free Press of Glencoe, 1961), pp. 19–26.

other than how one person feels about a general situation. Nor are statements of this kind likely to be based on much information. The polls illustrate that most people are perfectly willing to give their opinion about an issue even though they may know nothing about it. "Although tests of information invariably show at least 20 per cent of the public totally uninformed (and usually the figure is closer to 40 per cent), the 'no opinion' vote on any poll question seldom exceeds 15 per cent, and is often much lower. Mere lack of knowledge does not stop the public from offering opinions, a fact that is also revealed by the consistent finding that upwards of 10 per cent of those expressing a given attitude will answer 'don't know' when the interviewer asks them why they feel that way." [14]

Non-leaders, then, lack interest in and information about politics. As a result, politics is not discussed very much by non-leaders; but when it is discussed, the statements are colored by the biases of the speaker and revolve around opinions and evaluations. There is little attention to fact, and, just as important, an inability to see the relevance of politics to people's own interests.[15]

Politics as Democracy

The politics of democracy is characterized by leaders interacting with followers in a situation in which the followers elect the leaders. For our purpose, we shall limit our discussion to interaction occurring during campaigns, although there are other forms of interaction as well, for example, writing to a congressman, working for a political leader, and talking with a congressman. The latter activities, however, represent a very small proportion of the total interactions.

---

[14] Herbert H. Hyman and Paul B. Sheatsley, "The Current Status of American Public Opinion," in John C. Payne, ed., *The Teaching of Contemporary Affairs,* National Council for the Social Studies, 21st Yearbook, 1950, p. 16. Reprinted by permission of The National Council for the Social Studies.

[15] See Seymour M. Lipset, Paul F. Lazarsfeld, Allen H. Barton, and Juan Linz, "The Psychology of Voting: An Analysis of Political Behavior," in Gardner Lindzey, ed., *The Handbook of Social Psychology* (Reading, Mass.: Addison-Wesley Publishing Co., 1954), vol. 2, pp. 1124–1177. This analysis suggests that interest in politics is at least in part determined by the ability to see the relevance of politics to one's own interests.

Competitive elections are the hallmark of democracy. Robert Dahl, in a fascinating introduction to democratic theory, suggests that political parties and elections are two requisite institutions of any democracy. The former, which we shall discuss in the last chapter, provide for competition among leaders, and the latter provide the opportunity for non-leaders to choose among the leaders.[16] But what of the actual interaction situation during campaigns? How do leaders compete for the votes of non-leaders?

We can begin with what we already know about leaders and followers. Leaders are better informed and are more interested in material advantages for themselves and those whom they represent. Followers, on the other hand, are not well-informed—or even very interested in politics. They are mostly concerned with style issues about war and peace, prosperity and depression, corruption and "good" government. But the important distinction between leaders and followers in a campaign is that leaders are interested in getting re-elected. This means, of course, that in a two-party system they must appeal to as large a segment of their constituency as is possible.[17]

What kinds of pressures does the election process put on leaders? Appealing to large groups of people means that leaders must talk the language of followers, they must deal in "shoulds" and "oughts," they must deal in generalities and half-truths, they must say things they probably don't mean and don't understand themselves. Campaigns are attempts by nominees to do three things: [18]

1. Nominees attempt to reinforce their partisan followers. A candidate's major job is to maintain the party following. Losing strong partisan supporters to the other side would be an indication that a candidate was not faring well in the campaign. He must give his supporters something to cheer about, symbols to rally around, ammunition to use in discussions. This is why campaign rallies, although attended primarily by those who would vote for the candidate anyway, are so important. These rallies and television addresses serve to re-

[16] Robert A. Dahl, *A Preface to Democratic Theory* (Chicago: University of Chicago Press, 1956), Chap. 5.

[17] See Anthony Downs, *An Economic Theory of Democracy* (New York: Harper and Brothers, 1957), for an extended treatment of election politics. See especially Part II.

[18] Bernard Berelson, *et al., Voting*, Chap. 13, and Paul F. Lazarsfeld, Bernard Berelson, and Hazel Gaudet, *The People's Choice*, 2nd ed. (New York: Columbia University Press, 1948), *passim*.

inforce the choice of those who have already decided how they are going to vote. The candidate merely attempts to hold their vote. He attacks the opposition (and gets loud cheers); he makes loftly generalizations about what the future will be like with him and his party in office (and gets loud cheers); he tells a few jokes (and gets loud cheers); he waves his hand (and gets loud cheers). But this ritual is not devoid of meaning: it helps to cement the link between party supporters and the current candidate of that party.

2. Nominees attempt to activate the latent followers. Besides maintaining the current level of party support, a leader must also try to build a fire under those who would probably support him if they voted but who are not intense enough in their party loyalty to vote at every election. These people need to be prodded, to have their enthusiasm extended enough to make them think that the election is something important. Candidates use many means in an attempt to reach these potential supporters, including rallies, newspapers, radio and television, posters and billboards, direct-mail circulars, and so forth.

3. Nominees attempt to change those who support the other party. This is only a very small element in the campaign. Leaders are really not so much interested in changing votes as they are in reinforcing their supporters and activating their latent supporters. Nor are they very successful in changing votes. Most voting-behavior studies show that considerably less than ten per cent of the electorate changes parties from one election to the next.[19] Those who do change are those who are not highly committed to either party in the first place and do not have much interest in the election. They are difficult for the candidate to reach in his campaign, and are more likely to be prodded into voting for one candidate or the other through contact with family members, co-workers, or friends.[20] However, candidates do make broad appeals to the general population—appeals involving such issues as peace, prosperity, and clean government—which, if given persuasively, may corral a few votes from the opposition as well as reinforce and activate supporters.

Elections, then, are interactions among leaders and non-leaders, with the leaders wanting election to office as the outcome and non-leaders wanting to be reassured, entertained, and appealed to emo-

---

19 See, for example, Bernard Berelson, *et al., Voting,* Chap. 3.
20 Bernard Berelson, *et al.,* Voting, Chap. 7.

tionally. These two different kinds of needs lead to the result that speeches by candidates for office are highly ambiguous, general, and broad. Candidates must, first and foremost, not alienate any of their would-be supporters. They must appeal to a wide and diverse public, a public which is, generally speaking, uninformed and uninterested in specific issues. It is no wonder, then, that campaigns are generally devoid of any issue content (other than style issues), because they are primarily emotional appeals for support. Given the nature of the interaction situation and the characteristics of the actors, it is doubtful that it could be any other way.

Politics as Hierarchy

All political systems—even democratic systems—contain hierarchical politics. Politics as hierarchy is characterized by interaction among leaders and non-leaders in situations in which leaders are not elected by non-leaders. There are many examples of such situations, most of them in the form of bureaucratic organizations where it is necessary to establish a chain-of-command type of leadership in which power is unequally distributed, depending upon the nature of the task. The interactions which take place are not, as in bargaining and discussion, among peers, but among superordinates and subordinates. Unlike democracy, which is also characterized by interactions among leaders and non-leaders, hierarchy does not place the election of leaders in the hands of the followers. Leaders are recruited, rather, by appointment, promotion, tenure, and so forth.

Bureaucracies are usually task-oriented, that is, the organization is established for the purpose of accomplishing certain stated goals. These goals may be as diverse as crime detection, propaganda, preservation of forests, prosecution of anti-trust violations, and so forth. The organization is made up of members, each of whom performs a particular task oriented toward the major goal. Some members are put in charge of the work of others, and in turn are subordinate to someone higher in the organizational hierarchy.

But this, obviously, is not all there is to bureaucratic organizations. Many members within the organization are also attempting to achieve their own goals, for example, promotion, transfer to a "better" department, higher pay. The politics of hierarchy is really concerned with a whole series of sub-games within the organization. At times, the goals of individual members impede the attainment of the organizational goal. The politics of bureaucratic organizations is a fascinating study in and of itself.[21]

What is interesting, for our purposes, is the extent to which both employees and agents from outside the organization attempt to change hierarchical interactions into situations in which they are better able to deal. This is so much a part of the political process that it deserves special attention.

Often employees who wish to better their rank or who seek other advantages will try to change the "rules of the game" from leader-follower to friend-friend. It may be to their advantage, if they wish special privileges, to break the superordinate-subordinate relationship they began with in their job and establish a relationship on some other basis with those who are in a position to help them. They may, for example, attempt to transform the hierarchical relationship into a discussion situation in which their word carries as much weight as that of their superior. Or they may try to turn the relationship into one of bargaining. The subordinate is not completely without advantages which he can confer upon his superiors. His friendship, doing a "good" job (which would then reflect on the organization as a whole and on those in supervisory positions), and "inside" information about the organization which the leader may not be able to get in any other way are all resources which subordinates have at their disposal. In fact, the leader himself may be willing to relinquish a certain amount of his hierarchical control for just such benefits.

More important still are the attempts by outside organizations to influence bureaucratic leaders and to attempt to change the relationship from regulated to regulator. Many governmental agencies (and this is especially true of the so-called "independent" regulatory agencies) are put in a position of setting down rules and regulations governing a particular segment of the economy and the firms and

---

21 See Peter M. Blau, *The Dynamics of Bureaucracy* (Chicago: University of Chicago Press, 1955); Herbert A. Simon, *Administrative Behavior* (New York: Macmillan, 1947); Herbert A. Simon, Donald W. Smithburg, and Victor A. Thompson, *Public Administration* (New York: Alfred A. Knopf, Inc., 1950); and Leonard D. White, *Introduction to the Study of Public Administration,* 4th ed. (New York: The Macmillan Company, 1955).

other organizations involved. For example, the Federal Communications Commission is in charge of licensing radio and television stations and of establishing rules and regulations affecting the companies involved. With such political power as this, one could almost naturally expect attempts to influence the decisions of the Commission. Attempts are made to get individuals appointed to the Commission who will look favorably upon the needs and desires of the communication industry. The firms involved desire to change the relationship from regulator-regulated to one in which the regulated companies share in the decision-making processes.

Interactions between governmental agencies and individuals or organizations outside of government take place constantly. Often these attempts to influence governmental agencies take place through other elected or appointed officials acting as intermediaries. For example, congressmen are frequently calling agencies on behalf of their constituents. This is an integral part of politics. People want certain things and ask others to help them obtain them. Occasionally, these *ex parte* communications become major headlines, as in the Sherman Adams-Bernard Goldfine affair. Such relationships, however, need not involve gifts or other "suspicious" exchanges, and usually they do not. Many are merely calls from interested parties who are seeking information or who want to let the agency know that they are taking an interest. Direct pressure in the form of threats to reduce the agency's budget or attempts to bribe the decision-makers is the exception rather than the rule. Politics is much more subtle and complex than this. If pressure is brought to bear, it is usually indirect and implicit. And, since pressures usually come from all sides to a dispute, they often counteract one another.

Conclusion

Politics, then, is made up of a number of different political systems. We have explored in this chapter the politics of bargaining, discussion, democracy, and hierarchy. In the next chapter we shall be primarily concerned with how these four political systems are related to one another, and how people attempt to change the original decision-making process into a system from which they hope to receive increased benefits.

5

THE DISTRIBUTION OF

SYMBOLIC AND

MATERIAL REWARDS

In the last chapter we discussed four processes of decision-making and attempted to sketch out the kinds of relationships involved in each. In brief, the type of decision-making process involved in the distribution of advantages and disadvantages depends upon who is interacting with whom and under what conditions. When leaders interact with leaders, bargaining occurs; when non-leaders interact with non-leaders, the result is the process of discussion; when leaders interact with non-leaders, either hierarchy or democracy results, depending upon whether the positions of leadership are elective or not elective.

In this chapter we shall discuss three topics relevant to the distribution of payoffs in a political system: (1) the kinds of payoffs which are distributed, (2) who is interested in what kinds of payoffs, and (3) what factors are involved in changing the decision-making process from one type to another. Answers to each of these questions will aid us in arriving at an understanding of why politicians act the way that they do and why payoffs are distributed somewhat unequally.

A General Model of Politics

In this section we shall attempt to devise a simple model of politics which will connect the general relationships among different kinds of people, different kinds of decision-making processes, and different kinds of payoff distributions with which we have been dealing since Chapter 1. In the following sections we shall discuss in more detail the distribution of payoffs in each of the four decision-making systems.

First, people differ in the amount of issue-orientation they display in politics.[1] By "issue-orientation" is meant the range and number of issues which a person considers important and the amount of time he spends thinking, reading, and talking about them. Some people are highly issue-oriented; others are not. This difference in issue-orientation has a number of important consequences, many of which were introduced in Chapters 2 and 3.

1. The more issue-oriented a person is, the more his concern is with position rather than style issues.
   a. Conversely, the less issue-oriented a person is, the more his concern is with style rather than position issues.
2. The more a person's concern is with position issues, the more likely he is to be satisfied with material rewards.
   a. Conversely, the more a person's concern is with style issues, the more likely he is to be satisfied with symbolic rewards.
3. Therefore, the more issue-oriented a person is, the more likely he is to be satisfied with material rewards.
   a. Conversely, the less issue-oriented a person is, the more likely he is to be satisfied with symbolic rewards.

We shall remember that position issues are those issues having to do with specific and concrete problems, such as housing, subsidy programs, tariffs, and the like. Style issues are broad, moral questions, such as corruption, communism, and war. We have already elaborated upon this distinction in considerable detail in Chapter 2, and the reader is encouraged to glance back to refresh his memory.

---

[1] See Angus Campbell, Gerald Gurin, and Warren E. Miller, *The Voter Decides* (Evanston: Row, Peterson and Company, 1954), Chap. 8, and Angus Campbell, Philip Converse, Warren E. Miller, and Donald E. Stokes, *The American Voter* (New York: John Wiley and Sons, Inc., 1960), Chap. 8.

"Material and symbolic rewards" refers to the kinds of satisfactions that people receive from their interest in issues. Material rewards are those things that have an immediate and substantial impact on the lives of people (for example, lower interest rates, higher wages, and status benefits). "Symbolic rewards" are those things that reassure people, that calm their anxieties, and that appeal to their values and fears (for example, promises of "peace" and "prosperity"). Again, this distinction was elaborated in some detail in Chapter 2. The connection between the type of issue and the type of reward is that position issues are associated with material rewards; style issues, with symbolic rewards (see above).

Second, people differ in the kinds of attitudes they have. We have suggested, in Chapter 2, that attitudes may be classified into four types, depending upon the function being served for the individual: (1) utilitarian, (2) knowledge, (3) value-expressive, and (4) ego-defensive.[2] We suggest the following propositions based on this classification of attitudes:

1. The more issue-oriented a person is, the more likely it is that his attitudes about issues are serving a utilitarian or knowledge function.
   a. Conversely, the less issue-oriented a person is, the more likely it is that his attitudes about issues are serving a value-expressive or ego-defensive function.
2. Hence, those interested in position issues (highly issue-oriented people) will be more likely to have utilitarian and knowledge attitudes concerning issues.
   a. Conversely, those interested in style issues (people low in issue-orientation) will be more likely to have value-expressive and ego-defensive attitudes concerning issues.
3. Also, those with utilitarian and knowledge attitudes will be more interested in material rewards.
   a. Conversely, those with value-expressive and ego-defensive attitudes will be more interested in symbolic rewards.

There is a connection, then, between a person's issue-orientation (high or low), the kinds of attitudes he has regarding issues (utilitarian, knowledge, value-expressive, or ego-defensive), the types of issues in-

---

[2] See also, Daniel Katz, "The Functional Approach to the Study of Attitudes," *Public Opinion Quarterly,* vol. 24 (Summer, 1960), pp. 163–205.

volved (position or style), and the kind of rewards that will satisfy him (material or symbolic).

Third, as we have already suggested in Chapter 4, decision-making processes may be classified into four types: bargaining, hierarchy, discussion, and democracy. As we shall discuss further in later sections, bargaining and hierarchy are primarily concerned with the distribution of material advantages; discussion and democracy, with the distribution of symbolic advantages. Hence, we may draw the following generalizations:

1. Bargaining and hierarchy involve people with high issue-orientation, interest in position issues, utilitarian and knowledge attitudes regarding those issues, and interest in material rewards.

2. Discussion and democracy involve people with low issue-orientation, interest in style issues, value-expressive and ego-defensive attitudes regarding those issues, and interest in symbolic rewards.

Fourth, knowing whether people hold their attitudes predominantly for utilitarian and knowledge reasons or for value-expressive and ego-defensive reasons helps in the determination of what kinds of appeals will be useful in arousing and changing their attitudes.[3] Those who hold value-expressive and ego-defensive attitudes are subject to symbolic manipulation. Symbols and threats move these people into action, and "scare" tactics and utopian promises provide stimuli that arouse them. Those with utilitarian and knowledge attitudes, on the other hand, are less swayed by emotional and value-laden appeals. The concrete and material is much more important to them than the abstract and symbolic. These relationships will become clearer as we now begin to discuss each type of decision-making process as a system for distributing advantages and disadvantages. We shall also discuss the ways in which our "pure-type" decision-making processes become combinations and mixtures of two or more processes.

Bargaining

Bargaining is a relationship in which leaders interact with leaders. As such it is characterized by interactions among people who are highly issue-oriented, who are interested in position issues, who have

---

[3] Katz, "The Functional. . . ."

utilitarian and knowledge attitudes regarding those issues, who feel intensely about issues that affect them and the people they represent, and who are interested in retaining their own position of leadership. Leaders have many resources that they can bring to bear in their interactions with others, and they are highly informed about events and issues impinging upon themselves and those they represent.

Because those interacting in a bargaining situation may be characterized in the above fashion, the emphasis in bargaining is on the distribution of material advantages. Leaders attempt, in the bargaining situation, not only to cement their own positions of leadership vis-à-vis their group by achieving concrete, material rewards in the group's behalf: they also are looking out for material benefits that may come their way somewhat fortuitously. The motives of leaders center around things that they can achieve for themselves and their group. This fact places them in a position of having to be aware of issues and events that affect the group. Hence their high issue-orientation, interest in position issues, and so forth.

Bargaining tends toward hierarchy when the rules of bargaining become institutionalized, customary, or usual. When the participants involved in the bargaining relationship hold fixed positions, have certain well-defined roles, and acquire prestige for the role and esteem for themselves, then the rules of bargaining become fixed. A slightly different way of saying the same thing is that in certain interactions necessary to the final decision, some leaders have more potential power than others. One of the most interesting facets of such a situation is in the application of the "law of anticipated reactions." Participants in an institutionalized bargaining situation (such as Congress) learn to anticipate certain reactions from others and take steps, even before the others are brought into the process, to insure a favorable reaction. They may "water down" their proposals, or include benefits to those from whom unfavorable reactions are expected. They are, in effect, tacitly bargaining with those in positions to oppose and perhaps defeat the proposal. Interestingly enough, bargaining participants, before actual bargaining begins, may also demand more than they expect to receive in anticipation of having to make concessions. Both sides will want to claim "victory" in the negotiations and at the same time show their willingness to compromise.

Bargaining tends toward democracy to the extent that some participants in the bargaining relationship help to determine whether others will continue in their present positions. For example, many leader achieve bargaining power partially as a result of the large numbers o people they represent. If leaders are able to control the votes of their members (often the very fact that they are in a position to exer pressure on their members to vote one way or another is enough to make the threat of such control effective) and they use this potentia power as leverage in the bargaining process, then bargaining relation ships also involve democratic politics. For example, interest-group leaders may attempt to use their representation of members as leverage in bargaining with congressmen. To the extent that a congressman believes that the interest-group leader does in fact have some influence over the voting decisions of his members, to that extent bargaining i being transformed into a situation of democratic politics.

Discussion

Discussion is characterized by interaction among non-leaders. As a general rule, non-leaders are uninformed and uninterested in issues. As a consequence, issue-orientation is low, what interest there is tends to be concentrated on style issues, and the attitudes of the discussants tend to be value-expressive and ego-defensive. The politics of discussion is one of mutual exchange of opinions and beliefs. It is characterized by "attitude testing," that is, by people expressing their attitudes about various political events and personalities and seeing whether others agree or disagree with them. Since what is at stake is the participants' own egos and self-images (including their orientation toward their environment), and since discussions of politics among non-leaders are usually reserved for like-minded people,[4] the politics of discussion involves attempts to reach consensus or agreement and to avoid annoying disagreements and arguments. This is not to say that disagreements among participants in discussions are always avoided. When the parties are in disagreement and they feel intensely, discussion is likely to reinforce those disagreements. On the other hand, those who discuss issues are not likely to be in disagreement to begin with. For these reasons, the politics of discussion involves the distribution of symbolic advantages and disadvantages, that is, attempts to appeal to

---

[4] Bernard Berelson, Paul F. Lazarsfeld, and William N. McPhee, *Voting* (Chicago: University of Chicago Press, 1954), Chap. 6.

the emotions of others, the arousing or allaying of fears and anxieties, or the presentation of a person's values or self-image.

Discussion tends toward hierarchy in several circumstances. If the roles of the participants in the economic or social structure are on different status levels, then the opinions of the high-status participants are often given more weight than the opinions of the low-status participants. This fact follows from a number of considerations. For example, if a person is discussing politics with his boss or with someone he is trying to impress favorably, one way of creating a "good" impression is to support the other person's attitudes about various topics that are raised. This is another way of saying that often agreement is easier than disagreement, especially when other values are involved.

But there is a second, more interesting aspect of discussion involving the politics of hierarchy. Many studies have established the fact that non-leaders vary in the amount of information and interest they have in politics. Those high in these characteristics have been labeled "opinion leaders." [5] These are the people who participate most in political discussions, who tend to "lead" the discussions, who initiate the discussions, and whose opinions tend to prevail. Having greater information and interest, they are more attentive to political events and have thought about them more. So important is this fact that one study describes the flow of political information as a two-step process: from mass media to opinion leaders, and from opinion leaders to mass public. [6]

When there are opinion leaders among a group discussing politics, the situation is no longer characterized by the mutual flow of information and opinions among peers but becomes a rostrum in which a hierarchical system of discussion results. The opinion leaders take part more than do others, and their opinions and beliefs are likely to structure the discussion. It is to a person's advantage, of course, if he is interested in winning arguments (or simply wishing to be known as someone who is "informed" about political events), to try to change a situation of equal power to one of hierarchy if he is on top of the hierarchy. In politics, a person's superior level of information and

---

[5] Robert E. Lane, *Political Life* (New York: Free Press of Glencoe, 1959), pp. 52–56, summarizes much of the literature relating to opinion leaders.

[6] Elihu Katz and Paul F. Lazarsfeld, *Personal Influence* (New York: Free Press of Glencoe, 1955), pp. 3–4, 44–45.

interest is likely to make him an opinion leader almost by default, since others are low on both characteristics.

This situation has obvious consequences for group behavior. As was discussed in Chapter 3, group leaders are characterized by their higher level of interest and information, and they are able to command considerable power over group affairs as a result. When people abdicate from participation in group affairs, they naturally leave group decisions to those who participate, and leaders are just those who participate most. Lack of interest, then, seems to be a key factor in explaining why organizations tend toward hierarchy.

Democracy

In democratic politics, leaders must compete for the votes of non-leaders. This means that, periodically, leaders contend with one another over leadership positions, and non-leaders choose among the leaders vying for the positions. Non-leaders are quite heterogeneous in their interests, generally uninterested in any but style issues, characterized by value-expressive and ego-defensive attitudes, and uninformed. Leaders, of course, tend to be just the reverse. The strategy of the leaders is clear: make broad, vague, ambiguous, and emotional appeals in the hopes of winning as many votes as possible. This strategy serves a function for both leaders and non-leaders: for leaders, it is generally the only strategy that will result in success (given the nature of the electorate); to non-leaders it gives the kinds of things they want to hear. Campaigns help to assure non-leaders that they are making the "right" choice.

For these reasons democracy helps to distribute both material and symbolic advantages and disadvantages. Leaders contend for office, prestige, status, and, perhaps, economic comfort and security. For non-leaders, fewer direct, personal benefits are at stake. Non-leaders may perceive one candidate among those contending for office as helping them most. But such perceptions tend to be based on vague feelings of group interest or of good and bad.[7] And given the ambiguous and emotional appeals by leaders, clear perceptions by non-leaders of immediate personal gain are difficult to justify. During election time,

---

[7] Angus Campbell, *et al., The American Voter*, Chaps. 8, 9, and 10.

then, leaders are primarily concerned with material advantages surrounding the office they seek; non-leaders, with vague promises of a better life under one leader or party as opposed to another.

There are also, of course, "losers" in democratic politics in the sense that, for each office, only one candidate can win. For this reason, those leaders who are interested in material benefits for their members tend to stay out of campaigns, at least visibly. If their publicly endorsed candidate loses, they will obviously have a more difficult time achieving their goals through the candidate that won. For the most part, interest-group leaders (with some significant exceptions) prefer to carry on their activities between elections rather than during elections.[8]

When charismatic leadership develops, democracy tends toward hierarchy. *Charisma* is defined as an emotional bond between a leader and his followers. Hitler, Nasser, and Gandhi are examples of charismatic leaders. The leader, on the basis of his loyal following, may begin to act as though there were no opposition to his power. What opposition there is is often dealt with ruthlessly (for example, by Castro and Peron). Often an elaborate ideology is developed to justify "undemocratic" actions (such as the suspension of free elections), and scapegoats are used by the leader to cover up his mistakes or to rally the people behind him. Under such circumstances, the conditions of democracy no longer prevail and politics tends toward a rigidly hierarchical system.

Hierarchy

The politics of hierarchy is characterized by an emphasis on the distribution of material advantages and disadvantages. There are two reasons for this emphasis on material advantages. First, bureaucratic organizations deal directly with citizens who are interested in specific, concrete problems. Perhaps it is a licensing bureau or some agency regulating the affairs of a group. Bureaucrats are in a position to confer direct, personal benefits on their clients.

Second, much of the internal politics of hierarchical organizations, as well as external relations, is concerned with material advantages. Hierarchy is a decision-making process among leaders and non-leaders

---

8 David B. Truman, *The Governmental Process* (New York: Alfred A. Knopf, Inc., 1951), *passim*.

in situations in which non-leaders do not elect leaders. But often, in hierarchies, leaders do have something to say in the recruitment and advancement of non-leaders. In such a situation the subordinate members of the organization become aware of the impact of their actions on others, especially on the leadership.

Hierarchy tends toward bargaining when the external relations of the hierarchical organization are with leaders rather than non-leaders. The situation is no longer (as it is with non-leaders) one of bureaucrat versus citizen. It becomes a relationship in which both have something to offer—the bureaucrat, his service; the leader, his support of one kind or another. Congressmen, for example, control the purse-strings of bureaucratic organizations. It is in their power to cut or raise the organization's budget and do a thousand things which would make the life of the organization more comfortable. Congressmen, as well as other leaders, get the "red-carpet" treatment primarily because they have something to give in return for what they want.

With interest-group leaders the same is true. They are in a position to put pressure on bureaucrats, especially through their connections with other politicians, for example, congressmen. Since they, too, have something to offer in return for service, interest-group leaders are treated well by governmental bureaucracies.

Hierarchy is also related, in an interesting way, to democratic politics. This is illustrated in Professor Edelman's discussion of the relationships between the legislative and administrative branches of government in the distribution of material and symbolic advantages and disadvantages.[9] Professor Edelman suggests that most people in the mass public are satisfied that a problem is taken care of when the legislation involving that problem is passed. It is the legislative process that receives the most publicity—congressmen make gestures toward their constituents, politicians of all kinds issue public statements, public hearings are held, and so forth. After the legislation has been passed by Congress and signed into law by the President, public enthusiasm and concern subside. It is then, in the enforcement of the law, that organized groups have their greatest advantage over the unorganized public. The fact that a law is passed does not mean that it will be enforced, or that it will be interpreted as some proponents would like. It is after public enthusiasm has been spent and the issue is out of the

---

[9] Murray Edelman, "Symbols and Political Quiescence," *American Political Science Review*, vol. 54 (September, 1960), pp. 695–705.

headlines that organized groups are able to have their greatest impact on the administration and enforcement of the law.

Professor Edelman cites as an example the progressive income tax. Few pieces of legislation are so widely publicized and have such a wide following as an income tax law. Most people are aware that a progressive income tax (one in which the tax is figured on the basis of ability to pay) tends to benefit the poor to the disadvantage of the rich. But the public is not usually aware of the loopholes and ways of dodging paying taxes that are available to those who are able to take advantage of them. Family partnerships, income-splitting, multiple trusts, and percentage depletion are but a few of the devices open to well-to-do taxpayers to decrease their share of the tax burden and hence make the income tax less progressive than it is heralded to be. Trust-busting, protection against price discrimination, protection against deceptive trade practices, protection against excessive public utility charges, and tight control of union bureaucracies are other examples of situations in which legislative enactment and the administration and enforcement of law are often at variance.

Professor Edelman suggests a number of relationships, two of which are of particular interest:

1. "tangible resources and benefits are frequently not distributed to unorganized political group interests as promised in regulatory statutes and the propaganda attending their enactment," [10]

2. "the most intensive dissemination of symbols commonly attends the enactment of legislation which is most meaningless in its effects upon resource allocation." [11]

Edelman concludes that "successful political professionals have evidently long acted on the assumption that there is in fact relatively little familiarity [of voters with current public issues], that expressions of deep concern are rare, that quiescence is common, and that, in general, the congressman can count upon stereotyped reactions rather than persistent, organized pursuit of material interests on the part of most constituents." [12]

---

[10] Murray Edelman, "Symbols and . . .," p. 695. Reprinted by permission of the American Political Science Association.

[11] Murray Edelman, "Symbols and . . .," p. 697. Reprinted by permission of the American Political Science Association.

[12] Murray Edelman, "Symbols and . . .," p. 697. Reprinted by permission of the American Political Science Association.

Conclusion

Politics involves a number of complex relationships concerning people and decision-making processes. In order to describe and explain any complex phenomena, it is necessary to simplify and establish generalizations. This process of simplification takes the form of using concepts that abstract large "chunks" of the phenomena under study, stating relationships between and among the concepts, and then linking together the relationships in a logical fashion such that none contradicts others. This, in very brief form, is the process of building theory.

We have attempted, in this chapter, to offer the reader a tentative theory that can be used in understanding how politics, and more particularly American politics, works. We have summarized many of the generalizations made in previous chapters and have tried to relate how differences in people (their attitudes and resources), differences in issues, and differences in decision-making processes influence the distribution of advantages and disadvantages. To do this we have established concepts that we hope will be useful in describing the real world. On the basis of these concepts (for example, position and style issues, knowledge and ego-defensive functions of attitudes), we have attempted to develop generalizations that describe and explain relationships among the concepts. Finally, we have attempted to organize these relationships into a theory, that is, we have attempted to connect the relationships with each other. Table 2 summarizes the results of this process.

In the following chapter we shall employ our theory in the attempt to explain, more concretely, how specific American political institutions function.

TABLE 2   A GENERAL MODEL OF POLITICS

Type of Decision-Making	Actors	Interest and Information	Issue-Orientation	Type of Issue Concern	Type of Attitudes	Type of Rewards	System Changes
Bargaining	Leaders	High	High	Position	Utilitarian and Knowledge	Material	Hierarchy and Democracy
Discussion	Non-leaders	Low	Low	Style	Value-expressive and Ego-defensive	Symbolic	Hierarchy
Democracy	Leaders and non-leaders	High for leaders— low for non-leaders	High for leaders— low for non-leaders	Style	Utilitarian and Knowledge for leaders— Value-expressive and Ego-defensive for non-leaders	Material for leaders— Symbolic for non-leaders	Hierarchy
Hierarchy	Leaders and non-leaders	High	High	Position	Utilitarian and Knowledge	Material	Bargaining

6

SOME DESCRIPTIONS

AND GENERALIZATIONS

In this chapter we shall explore six institutions in American politics and, using the theory we have already discussed, describe how they operate. The main emphasis will be placed on how these institutions are organized, the kinds of decision-making processes that are carried on within and among them, the kinds of payoffs that are distributed, and to whom payoffs are distributed. We shall discuss Congress, the Presidency, the Supreme Court, the election process, political parties, and interest groups, in that order.

Congress

The most important characteristic of Congress is its decentralization of political power.[1] This fact is the result of three important factors.

---

[1] For excellent discussions of Congress, see Bertram M. Gross, *The Legislative Struggle* (New York: McGraw-Hill Book Company, 1953); William H. Riker, *Democracy in the United States* (New York: The Macmillan Company, 1953), Chap. 5; and Roland Young, *The American Congress* (New York: Harper and Brothers, 1958).

First, congressional parties are weak.[2] Party leaders have few controls over party members in Congress. Unlike the English Parliament, where party leaders have a number of formal and informal means of insuring legislative support from party members in Parliament, party leaders in Congress have few sanctions at their disposal, especially outside of Congress itself, to "punish" party members who do not vote with the leadership. Majority and minority leaders can threaten to withhold such prizes as committee assignments, but their influence even here is limited by the rules of seniority and other factors.[3]

A second factor that promotes decentralization of political power in Congress, and that is related to the weakness of congressional parties, is the factor of district representation. Congressmen are elected from districts and owe their election to the interests and people in those districts. For example, in the House of Representatives there are 435 congressmen representing as many districts. We would expect to find, and do find, these districts varying considerably in size and kinds of interests. Since there are only two major parties, we would also expect there to be considerable overlap in the kinds of constituencies that the parties represent. Democrats do not all come from large, urban areas, for example. There are many small, rural areas that have Democratic representatives. The same is true for the Republicans: the districts that their congressional members represent vary from rural to urban, business to farm, and so forth.[4] Since congressmen must win election in their own constituencies, they are inclined to pay attention to the interests within their districts, especially if the interests are vocal and persistent. Since these districts are so varied, even within parties, it is difficult for the leadership to establish a party program and to expect all party members to follow it. Re-election at home in fact may depend upon *independence* from party programs that affect certain districts adversely.

---

2 For a detailed description of party voting in Congress, see David B. Truman, *The Congressional Party* (New York: John Wiley and Sons, Inc., 1959).

3 See George Goodwin, Jr., "The Seniority System in Congress," *American Political Science Review*, vol. 53 (June, 1959), pp. 412–437; and Nicholas A. Masters, "House Committee Assignments," *American Political Science Review*, vol. 55 (June, 1961), pp. 345–358.

4 For a discussion of rural-urban differences, see Gordon E. Baker, *Rural Versus Urban Political Power* (New York: Random House, 1955).

A third factor related to decentralization in Congress is the fact that Congress is organized by a committee system. There are twenty-one Standing Committees in the House and seventeen in the Senate. There are many more subcommittees—over one hundred in both houses. Almost all legislation is referred to committees before debate on the floor of Congress, and, in the main, these committees have the power to kill, modify, or report out unchanged legislation referred to them. Committee and subcommittee chairmen, in turn, have considerable influence over the business of their particular committees. They schedule or do not schedule meetings of the committee; they set the agenda for committee discussion; they schedule witnesses at committee hearings; and they preside over the discussion. These functions place a great deal of potential power in the hands of a relatively few congressmen on any given issue, but the composition of those in leadership positions changes from issue to issue.

Because of this high degree of decentralization, policy is made mostly by bargaining. There are many leaders in Congress, each with a particular position in the decision-making process and each possessing certain prerogatives and powers. It is necessary, in sending a bill through Congress, to go through a rather complex procedure in which many leaders with certain powers must be consulted (for example, the Speaker, party leaders, and committee and subcommittee chairmen). Because of their differing backgrounds and constituent interests, not all of those who are consulted will feel the same way about a particular piece of legislation. Hence, it will be necessary to compromise and make concessions, to modify the bill, to add to it and subtract from it, so that it will be in line with the preferences of as many members as is necessary for its adoption (usually, a simple majority), including the most influential leaders, who are able to halt and slow up legislation that does not appeal to them.

As in any bargaining relationship, material advantages and disadvantages are exchanged. Not only is this true with respect to the content of the bill (for example, the insistence by representatives of dairy areas that subsidies for milk products be included in a general farm program); it is also true of political support as well. For example, in battles over the adoption of rules of procedure or specific legislation in either house of Congress, the participants are not only aware that the outcome will affect the likelihood that their preferences concerning the content of legislation will prevail, but they also realize that a power struggle within the chamber itself is taking place between the parties and among various factions within the parties. The outcome determines the relative power advantages of the participants as well as the content of legislation.

But what of the distribution of payoffs? Who gets what in congressional decision-making? Generally, we may say that legislation need not have majority support with respect to content. Because of the existence of many points in Congress where small minorities may obstruct and impede legislation (a consequence of decentralized decision-making), decision-makers are placed in position to demand support from others on one bill in exchange for support on other bills. This is the process of "logrolling" discussed in Chapter 4. Those supporting particular bills must build coalitions that add up to majority support and that include many of the most influential leaders. But this support need not necessarily result from agreement over the content of the bill. Since congressional constituencies are small, and since they vary in interests, not all members of Congress will have a position on any given bill or feel the same degree of intensity about it. There will be many who are apathetic on different issues. As was indicated in Chapter 4, logrolling is a useful way to build coalitions with those who are apathetic.

We can, however, be more specific with respect to the kinds of interests that Congress is most likely to support. Congress, for reasons that we shall discuss, does not accurately represent all segments of the American population. Some interests tend to be over-represented; others are under-represented. This situation is the result of factors involved in the election of members. Generally speaking, Congress tends to over-represent the interests located in three kinds of constituencies.

First, Congress tends to over-represent the interests located in sparsely populated states. There are two Senators from each state regardless of any state's population. This means that a sparsely populated state such as Nevada has as many Senators as a state with a large population such as New York. For example, Robert Dahl finds that "the eight largest states with 54 per cent of the voters [based on the 1952 election for members of the House of Representatives] have the same number of votes in the Senate as the eight smallest states with less than 3 per cent of the voters." [5] Also, "a majority of votes in th Senate can be cast by Senators representing less than 15 per cent c the voters." [6]

Second, Congress tends to over-represent the interests in one-part states and districts. One-party areas tend to be over-represented be cause positions of power in Congress (e: ecially committee chairman ships) are at least partially determined   seniority (length of service) Those areas that can continue to retur   heir representatives (usuall one-party areas) will be more likely   ive senior members in Con gress and hence gain positions of power. Those in positions of power of course, have more resources with wh h to bargain and hence ar able to make more demands.

Third, Congress tends to over-represer   the interests located in rura states and areas. Many investigators h: e shown that congressiona districts are malapportioned in favor o ural areas.[8] During the las 50 years, there has been a great populati n shift from rural to urba areas. Whereas in 1910, 45.7 per cent of t e population lived in urba areas, in 1960 the figure rose to 63.0 per ent.[9] State legislatures, how ever, have been slow to redistrict congi essional seats to match th changing character of the districts. Hence rural areas have many mor seats than their population would entitl them to have if districting were done solely on the basis of populati n.

Also, as Table 3 illustrates, these thi e factors tend to reinforce one another. That is, one-party and modified one-party states tend tc be less heavily populated and more rural than are two-party states.

---

[5] Robert A. Dahl, *A Preface to Democratic Theory* (Chicago: University of Chicago Press, 1956), p. 116. Copyright, 1956, by the University of Chicago. Reprinted by permission.

[6] Robert A. Dahl, *A Preface . . .*, p. 116. Copyright, 1956, by the University of Chicago. Reprinted by permission.

[7] George Goodwin, Jr., "The Seniority System . . .," pp. 425–426, and Lester W. Jackson, *District Safety, Seniority, and Chairmanships in the House of Representatives* (unpublished master's thesis, University of Wisconsin, 1961).

[8] V. O. Key, Jr., *Politics, Parties, and Pressure Groups* (New York: Thomas Y. Crowell Company, 1958), 4th ed., pp. 328 ff.; Robert A. Dahl, *A Preface . . .*, Chap. 4; and Gordon E. Baker, *Rural Versus . . .*, passim.

[9] Under the old definition of *urban area*. Under the new definition, the figure is 69.9 per cent urban. *United States Statistical Abstract*, 1961, Department of Commerce, Bureau of the Census, p. 23.

TABLE 3   RELATIONSHIP BETWEEN ONE-PARTY AND MODIFIED ONE-PARTY STATES, TWO-PARTY STATES, AND SIZE OF POPULATION AND PERCENTAGE URBAN

Type of Party System *	Mean Population **	Mean Per Cent Urban **
One-Party and Modified One-Party States (22)...	3,186,590	53.1
Two-Party States (26)....	4,138,281	69.4

* Austin Ranney and Willmoore Kendall, *Democracy and the American Party System* (New York: Harcourt, Brace and Company, 1956), Ch. 7. One-party states are: Alabama, Arkansas, Florida, Georgia, Louisiana, Mississippi, South Carolina, Texas, Vermont, and Virginia. Modified one-party states are: Iowa, Kansas, Kentucky, Maine, New Hampshire, North Carolina, North Dakota, Oklahoma, Oregon, Pennsylvania, South Dakota, and Tennessee. The remainder are two-party states. These figures exclude Alaska and Hawaii.
** United States Census of Population: 1960. United States Department of Commerce, Bureau of the Census.

This over-representation of sparsely populated, one-party, rural states means that, in the bargaining process, the interests from these states tend to have a greater advantage than their numbers would ordinarily allow. This has a number of important consequences for executive-congressional relations that we shall take up after we discuss the organization of the Presidency.

The Presidency

The Presidency, like Congress, is also a decentralized political organization. It is a mistake to view the President as head of a hierarchical organization with power flowing downward and those under the President merely carrying out his orders.[10] True, the President does make a number of policy decisions that parts of the vast bureaucracy technically under his control are then ordered to put into effect, but these decisions are not made by the President in isolation.

---

10 For an elaboration of this point see Richard E. Neustadt, *Presidential Power* (New York: John Wiley and Sons, Inc., 1960).

The President receives advice from many sources, including those who are subordinate to him. Also, the very size of the Executive Office and the Departments over which he exercises jurisdiction places several important limitations on the decision-making power of the President:

1. The work being carried on within the bounds of the Presidency is too large for any one man to oversee constantly.
2. The President himself has limited resources in terms of time and energy.
3. Therefore, the President must delegate authority and responsibility to others and concentrate, personally, on only a few of the most important issues.
4. This gives the men under the President vast discretion over many important areas that require attention.

It is easy to see, then, how decisions are made by a number of subordinates to the President and how this decentralized decision-making organization could spawn bargaining situations (for example, in the allocation of scarce resources among various departments and bureaus).

The President also "loses control" of his "hierarchical organization" in the sense that Presidential appointees to high-level offices (for example, Assistant Secretaries and above in the various Departments) tend to be chosen after consultation with those interests in the population that will be most affected by the decisions handed down by the Departments in question. Generally speaking, the various high-level officials in our government are chosen with the approval of the groups with which they will be most in contact. These men develop close working associations with the representatives of such interests. Also, there are other factors that tend to make political appointees independent of the President. Some statutes place responsibility for certain decisions in the hands of cabinet officials, not of the President. Also, political appointees may develop friendships and close alliances with influential congressmen. Because of these factors it often becomes politically difficult (although legally feasible) to fire a Cabinet or sub-Cabinet member who does not share the President's preferences. When such men become politically "non-fireable," one can easily see what effect this might have on the supposedly hierarchical relationships between the President and his subordinates. Such a hierarchical relationship readily turns into a relationship of bargaining, with the

'resident having to bargain with his own subordinates to get what
e wants.

The President, of course, has at his command a number of resources
hat lesser officers of the government do not have to make his position
uperior in potential power.[11] One of the most important is his public
restige. He also, of course, has a great number of material benefits
o distribute, such as patronage. Hence the relationship is not that of
quals—but neither is it entirely that of superior-subordinate.

Like Congress, the President tends to over-represent constituents
rom certain parts of the country. This result is due primarily to the
nanner in which he is elected. It may at first glance appear as though
he Electoral College, since it gives to each state the same number of
lectors as it has congressmen and Senators, would favor the same
nterests as does Congress. For example, Alaska, with a population of
ipproximately 228,000, has 3 electoral votes, and New York, with a
oopulation of approximately 16,827,000, has 43 electoral votes. This
;ives Alaska 1 electoral vote for every 76,000 people, and New York
electoral vote per 391,000 people. But this would be true only if the
:andidates received the same proportion of electoral votes as they re-
:eive popular votes. Because of the unit rule in the Electoral College
(the candidate with the largest number of votes in the state wins all
of the electoral votes for that state), each voter in Alaska is influencing
:he disposition of only 3 electoral votes, whereas in New York each
voter is influencing the disposition of 43 electoral votes. So important
does the unit rule of the Electoral College make the electoral votes of
large states that a candidate may become President by winning only
a plurality of votes in the eleven largest states and losing all the other
states.

Because of the systematic distortion of popular votes by the Electoral
College, then, the President tends to over-represent the interests located
in the following three kinds of constituencies:

First, the President tends to over-represent the interests located in
populous states. Those states with the largest blocs of electoral votes
contribute most heavily to the victory of the winning candidate. This
fact has three very important consequences, all of which contribute to
the over-representation of large states. First, those states which contribute most heavily to victory are likely to be rewarded for having

---

11 Neustadt, *Presidential Power, passim.*

done so. Second, presidential and vice-presidential candidates of bot
parties tend to come from states with large electoral votes. This, c
course, is an aid to the candidate in winning that state for the part:
Since a candidate has to come from some state, why not one with
large bloc of electoral votes? Third, candidates tend to campaig
most heavily in populous states and are likely to make most of thei
promises and do most of their bargaining—programs for votes—i
those states.

Second, the President tends to over-represent the interests in two
party states. Two-party states, by definition, are marginal in presi
dential politics, that is, they can, and do, go to either party. This, c
course, is another reason why candidates spend much of their tim
campaigning in the populous states (as Table 4 illustrates, two-part
states and populous states tend to be the same). Not only is thei
electoral vote large; it is "uncertain" as well.

Third, the President tends to over-represent the interests located i:
urban states. Table 4 also shows that populous states tend to be no
only two-party states but also more highly urban than the less populou
states. This means, of course, that candidates for the Presidency spen:

**TABLE 4   RELATIONSHIP BETWEEN SIZE OF POPULATION, PER CENT URBAN
AND TWO-PARTYNESS OF STATES**

	Total Electoral College Vote *	Mean Per Cent Urban **	Percentage of States Classified as Two-Party **
Eleven Most Populous States ** ..	268	77.7	73%
All Other States	267	57.3	49%

* The Electoral College vote for each state represents the number o:
electoral votes that each state will be able to cast in the 1964 election
assuming a House of Representatives membership of 435. This datun
draws attention to the fact that the eleven most populous states have
sufficient electoral votes to elect the President even if the remaining 3!
states unite on another candidate.

** United States Census of Population: 1960. United States Departmen
of Commerce, Bureau of the Census. The eleven most populous state:
are, in the order of size: New York, California, Pennsylvania, Illinois
Ohio, Texas, Michigan, New Jersey, Massachusetts, Florida, and In
diana. The data for "All Other States," except for the Electoral Col
lege vote, exclude Alaska and Hawaii.

*** Austin Ranney and Willmoore Kendall, *Democracy and the American
Party System* (New York: Harcourt, Brace and Company, 1956), Chap.
7.

, great deal of their campaign time in urban centers in the populous, two-party states. Again, spending time there means that campaign pledges will attempt to attract the support of the voters in these urban areas.

As is now clear from our investigation into who is likely to get what in Presidential and congressional decision-making, the constituencies that the President tends to over-represent are just the opposite from the constituencies that Congress tends to over-represent. That is, Congress tends to over-represent small, rural, one-party states; the President, large, urban, two-party states. This difference produces a "natural" conflict between the President and Congress. In their legislative bargaining, the President and Congress are, at the outset, at odds with one another owing to the opposite over-representations that factors in the electoral process tend to create. This means that, even when the President and Congress are controlled by the same political party, it will be difficult for the President to get his legislative program through Congress. Since public laws need the approval of both Congress and the President, the need to avoid a stalemate through bargaining and compromise is readily apparent.

The Supreme Court

First and foremost, the Supreme Court is a political body. The decisions that it makes are political because they affect a large number of people, and they affect them differently. Supreme Court decisions influence a wide range of values, involve large payoffs, affect intense values of people, and are, for varying lengths of time, relatively binding and irreversible. With almost every Supreme Court decision, advantages are distributed unequally among the population.[12]

For example, in 1954 when the Supreme Court decided that "separate but equal" schools for Negroes were unconstitutional, few would argue that this was not a political decision advantaging Negroes in the population and running counter to the preferences of many whites, especially in the South. In fact, in many respects the Supreme Court may be looked upon as a legislative body making decisions in areas

---

12 For excellent introductions to Supreme Court decision-making, see Jack W. Peltason, *Federal Courts in the Political Process* (New York: Random House, 1955); and Glendon A. Schubert, *Constitutional Politics* (New York: Holt, Rinehart, and Winston, 1960).

that Congress, in conjunction with the President, finds it difficult to make. Many political disputes are thrown into the lap of the Supreme Court because the "normal" legislative process (that is, Congress and the President) is unable to act to redress the grievances and satisfy the needs of certain people.[13]

Second, the Supreme Court is subject to pressures by groups as is any other political body.[14] In any form of government, one can predict that wherever there is a decision-making body that makes decisions involving the lives of many people, and when these decisions affect different people differently, there will be attempts by at least some of the people involved in the issue to resolve it in their own favor. Democracies and dictatorships differ in the number and kind of groups that are allowed to make demands, not in the fact that there are people making them.[15]

The most obvious way in which interest groups attempt to influence public policy made by the Court is in bringing cases before it and arguing for a favorable decision. American law is governed by the adversary process, in which those in a dispute (the litigants) appear in court (one party as plaintiff, the other as defendant) for the purpose of persuading the court to rule in their favor. Many pressure groups support, financially and otherwise, certain kinds of litigants asking for a redress of grievances. For example, the National Association for the Advancement of Colored People initiates in federal and state courts many cases involving the rights of Negroes, and is quite prepared to appeal an adverse decision all the way to the Supreme Court. The American Civil Liberties Union is a "liberal" organization which supports many litigants involved in cases concerning such issues as freedom of speech, press, and assembly. Interest groups may also file *amicus curiae* briefs in cases in which they are interested in the hopes of influencing the decision of the court.[16]

---

[13] See David B. Truman, *The Governmental Process* (New York: Alfred A. Knopf, Inc., 1951), Chap. 15.

[14] Clement E. Vose, "Litigation as a Form of Pressure Group Activity," *The Annals of the American Academy of Political and Social Science,* vol. 319 (September, 1958), pp. 20–31.

[15] See Robert A. Dahl, *A Preface . . .,* Chap. 5, for a more elaborate statement of this proposition.

[16] Clement E. Vose, "Litigation as a Form . . ."; and Glendon A. Schubert, *Quantitative Analysis of Judicial Behavior* (New York: Free Press of Glencoe, 1959), Chap. 2.

Third, appointments to the Supreme Court involve much the same kind of "politics" as do other kinds of political appointments. For example, interest groups are vitally concerned with who sits on the Court bench. What kinds of values, beliefs, and attitudes Supreme Court Justices have are important factors in determining the decisions that will be handed down on controversial issues.[17] One example will serve to illustrate these generalizations.

During the past several years the Supreme Court has tended to split 5 to 4 on many so-called "liberal-conservative" issues (such as First Amendment freedoms) in favor of the conservatives. The votes have usually been Frankfurter, Clark, Harlan, Whittaker, and Stewart on the conservative side, and Warren, Black, Douglas, and Brennan on the liberal side. President Kennedy's appointment of Byron White to take the place of Justice Whittaker, who resigned in April, 1962, because of ill health, may tend to swing the balance 5 to 4 in favor of the liberals (assuming no other changes). However, predictions of this nature are extremely difficult to make. Although Presidents usually attempt to appoint individuals to the Court who share their views on important issues likely to come before the Court, more than one President has been disappointed in his choice. The most recent example is President Eisenhower's appointment in 1953 of Earl Warren as Chief Justice, who turned out to be considerably more liberal than President Eisenhower would have liked.

Supreme Court appointments, like other government appointments, involve political issues. Hence, a number of questions about the prospective Justice are usually taken into consideration. Such factors as his political party affiliation, his public and private stands on various issues that are likely to come before the Court, his relationship with the Senators and party leaders from his home state, recommendations from the American Bar Association and other interested parties—all these and more are factors that help to determine who gets appointed to the Court. Also, appointments to the Court must be approved by a majority in the Senate, and the nomination must first go through the Senate Judiciary Committee. The likelihood of a candidate surviving these ratifying procedures is also taken into consideration in the appointment process.

What of the payoffs in Supreme Court decision-making? Who is

---

[17] See Glendon A. Schubert, *Quantitative Analysis . . .*, *passim.*

likely to be advantaged and who disadvantaged? This is an extremely difficult question, and only a partial answer can be sketched here. First, let us note that the decisions of the Supreme Court are rarely enforced by force or coercion. Little Rock is an exception to a long history of examples that prove the rule. Rather, the Court depends upon public acceptance of its decisions and the myth that the nine justices on the Court are dispensing "justice," not payoffs. Hence we have a situation in which it is extremely difficult (and sometimes dangerous) for the Court to hand down opinions that are not shared by large segments of the population.

For example, Robert Dahl suggests that the Court is not the protector of minority rights that some people like to think it is. Dahl points out that there is no case on record in which the Supreme Court has declared a federal law unconstitutional because it interfered with freedom of religion, speech, press, or assembly.[18] On the basis of the evidence carefully presented, Dahl concludes that "the policy views dominant on the Court are never for long out of line with the policy views dominant among the lawmaking majorities of the United States." [19] The strongest factor contributing to this conclusion, Dahl suggests, is the ability of the President to appoint new justices. "Over the whole history of the Court, on the average one new justice has been appointed every twenty-two months. Thus a President can expect to appoint about two new justices during one term of office; and if this were not enough to tip the balance on a normally divided Court, he is almost certain to succeed in two terms." [20]

The Supreme Court, then, in its policy-making function, normally hands down decisions that are congruent with the current law-making majority. As we would expect, however, since the personnel on the Court may not change as rapidly as the law-making majority (President and Congress), there may be periods in which the Court and the "normal" legislative process are in conflict. As Dahl points out, however, even though the Court may hold out for long periods of time

---

[18] Robert A. Dahl, "Decision-Making in a Democracy: The Supreme Court as a National Policy-Maker," *Journal of Public Law*, vol. 6 (Fall, 1957), p. 292.

[19] Robert A. Dahl, "Decision-Making . . .," p. 285. Reprinted by permission of the Emory University Law School.

[20] Robert A. Dahl, "Decision-Making . . .," p. 284. Reprinted by permission of the Emory University Law School.

(for example, on child-labor laws), it never can "win," primarily because "it" eventually changes in personnel.

In summary, we can view the Supreme Court as a policy-making body. It is a dispenser of advantages and disadvantages on a number of important political questions. When we say that a decision by the Court is "just" or "unjust," what we mean is that either we agree or we disagree with the decision (when we have a preference one way or the other) or, lacking preferences, we feel that it is "rational" and "fitting" that the Court arrived at the decision it did. There is also, of course, a strong feeling of veneration toward the Supreme Court as a political institution. Indeed, the Court attempts to encourage this feeling by casting its decisions primarily in moral and value-laden terms. There are, of course, material advantages and disadvantages being distributed in most cases before the Court. The parties to the dispute are intense; the decision-making process is one involving bargaining. However, in order to discourage widespread dissatisfaction with its decisions, the Court often hands down ambiguous and vague opinions. This is true of position issues that reach the Court as well as style issues. Because position issues can involve large and immediate benefits to many people, and because the Court has to rely on public acceptance and Presidential and congressional support for its decisions, the Supreme Court is often placed in a position of having to skirt the issue or to cast its opinion in symbolic rather than material terms.

Style and Position Issues in Democratic Bargaining

The three governmental institutions discussed above are concerned primarily with the distribution of material advantages and disadvantages and may be chiefly characterized as bargaining decision-making processes. *Primarily* and *chiefly* are used advisedly in these two generalizations, since symbolic advantages are involved in the democratic aspect of politics within these institutions (see the previous chapter). That is, when governmental officials make public statements about their actions, they tend to cast their statements in terms of "the public interest." Presidential press conferences, interviews with congressmen and congressional speeches, and written opinions by the

Justices on the Supreme Court are good examples of politicians in administrative, legislative, and judicial proceedings addressing the public in primarily general, vague, and moral terms. Appeals to "the national interest," "what's good for the country," and such abstract categories as "freedom," "liberty," and "justice" are employed with the effect that the bulk of the public rarely is aware of anything but symbolic advantages.

Sometimes such statements are employed because vague, general, and moral issues are at stake. That is, some issues which come before Congress, the President, or the Supreme Court are, in fact, style issues that are directly concerned with the distribution of symbolic advantages and disadvantages. Discussions involving the economic state of the country, or whether the United States should recognize Red China, are such issues. These issues are no less "real" than are position issues; they are merely concerned with broad, general, and ambiguous problems rather than specific and concrete ones. People are likely to be "for" or "against" such questions, or to believe that we are or are not in a "recession" and in danger of a "depression," on a variety of grounds having to do with what they consider to be "right" or "wrong," "good" or "bad," or on the basis of various fears and anxieties. There are times, however, when leaders (both governmental and non-governmental) attempt to justify their own preferences concerning the material distribution of advantages and disadvantages by appealing to general and moral principles. Attempts by leaders of interest groups to justify such material advantages as protective tariffs, federal subsidies, or higher wages in terms of the "good of the country" are examples of using style issues and talking about the distribution of symbolic advantages when, in fact, position issues and material advantages are at stake.

Interestingly enough, the reverse of using style issues to cloak material advantages also occurs in politics. That is, there are professional "gossips" who constantly look for the "hidden" private interests that they think lie behind all political statements and actions as though the distinction between position and style issues did not exist. For example, on the question of building bomb shelters as a safeguard against nuclear war, some observers look for the connection between such an issue and certain economic ties. Politicians who favor the building of such shelters (especially through private enterprise) are charged with cooperating with cement producers and bomb-shelter manufacturers. Occasionally this might be the case. It is also true that if a bomb-shelter program gets under way (that is, if the now essentially style issue of bomb shelters gets beyond the initial stage of "should we or shouldn't we" into the stage of "how many and how much"), a number of people will make money. But this does not mean that the only reason we shall have a bomb-shelter program is the fact that certain "insidious" interests are merely looking for profit. A great many people feel, and will continue to feel, that it is in the "national interest" to have such a program. They are still operating on the style level and are not trying to hide private interests. We must be careful to distinguish those who use style issues for their own purposes from those who are interested in style issues for their own sake.

However, it is true that most politicians, at one time or another, use the public's concern with style issues for their own purposes. They may do so under two conditions. First, as we have already mentioned, they may be attempting to justify other interests. They do so by cloaking private motives under the garb of "justice," "freedom," and so forth. Or, second, politicians may attempt to appeal to the public when they are losing a fight. They may attempt to increase the scope of the conflict and place it in an arena in which they feel that they will have a better chance of winning.[21] As an example, Presidents who are having difficulty getting their programs through Congress may take to radio and television for the purpose of drumming up support for legislation that Congress is slow to approve, in the hopes that constituents will apply pressure on their congressmen. They will make such appeals essentially in style terms because, as we shall see as we discuss election politics, such a strategy seems more likely than any other to be successful.

Congress, the President, and the Supreme Court, then, are primarily concerned with the distribution of material advantages and disadvantages, but not exclusively. Style issues do concern the decision-makers in these governmental institutions, and symbolic advantages and disadvantages are involved in many of their decisions. In the next two sections we shall concentrate on two non-governmental institutions that are primarily "in business" to distribute symbolic advan-

---

21 E. E. Schattschneider, *The Semisovereign People* (New York: Holt, Rinehart, and Winston, 1960), Chap. 1.

tages and disadvantages. We shall discuss reasons why this is the case—reasons that will also shed some light on why politicians deal with the public primarily on the symbolic level. In the next section we shall discuss the election process, and in the section following we shall discuss political parties.

The Election Process

Most elected politicians are interested in getting re-elected to public office. To do so they must receive more votes than their opponents. These two facts, plus the knowledge that, generally speaking, people are (1) poorly informed about issues, (2) not much interested in politics, and (3) vote mainly on the basis of their party identification,[22] give rise to the consideration of electoral strategies by office-seekers for the purposes of getting elected. Since we have already discussed parts of this question in Chapter 4, we shall, here, briefly outline three major strategies used in elections.

1. Strategy number one is to be general. The electorate to which a candidate must appeal for support, especially in a two-party system, is large and diverse. The main task of the candidate is to reinforce and activate those who already identify themselves with the candidate's party.[23] This latent support for the candidate ranges considerably over social classes, ethnic and religious groups, occupational strata, and so forth.[24] Candidates must, therefore, phrase their public statements so that they appeal to all or most of this large and diverse audience. The more specific candidates become on issues, the more likely it is that: (1) they will lose the attention of most of their audience, since most will not be interested in specific issues; and (2) they will be appealing to the interests of only a small segment of that audience.

2. Electoral strategy number two is to be vague. This second

---

[22] See Bernard Berelson, Paul F. Lazarsfeld, and William N. McPhee, *Voting* (Chicago: University of Chicago Press, 1954) ; Angus Campbell, Gerald Gurin, and Warren E. Miller, *The Voter Decides* (Evanston: Row, Peterson and Company, 1954) ; and Angus Campbell, Philip E. Converse, Warren E. Miller, and Donald E. Stokes, *The American Voter* (New York: John Wiley and Sons, Inc., 1960).

[23] See Chap. 4, "Politics as Democracy" section.

[24] Bernard Berelson, *et al., Voting;* Angus Campbell, *et al., The Voter Decides;* and Angus Campbell, *et al., The American Voter.*

strategy follows from the notion that most candidates attempt not to "lose" any votes already predisposed in their favor or to alienate large segments of the population. This is especially true of candidates, whether Republican or Democratic, who are behind in the pre-election estimates of popular support. Candidates who are running ahead can better afford to antagonize voters. Being clear about issues would run the risk of (1) being too "technical" and talking "above the heads" of the voters, and (2) having yourself understood by segments in the population who will disagree with what they understand.

Hence candidates concentrate on general issues—usually style issues, such as corruption in government, communism, staying out of war, and the prosperity-depression "syndrome"—and make rather vague appeals concerning them, for example, "moving forward in the 60's" or "we can't stand pat." These "stands" on "issues," of course, are designed to "take in" as much of the electorate as possible.

3. Electoral strategy number three is to tell people what they want to hear. The strategies we are discussing here are not, at least very often, deliberate attempts by candidates to "fool" the public, at least in the sense that candidates have other alternatives. The basic reason why candidates deal in general and vague statements and slogans is that other alternatives are likely to lead to defeat. Candidates are interested in winning, and they will use the "best" strategies available. If being specific and clear about issues and problems would get them elected more readily than other alternatives, they would certainly engage in their use. But, as we have already said a number of times, people's lack of interest in and information about politics and political issues forces the politician to use these facts about the electorate to his own advantage. If he doesn't, his opponent will. The issues in which people are most interested are those things that they are likely to discuss among themselves: style issues and the personal qualities of candidates. Voters, for better or worse, like to be told that X candidate will "make a better life" for them. This is the kind of campaign that most people are prepared to listen to and watch, and this is the kind of campaign they get.

These considerations lead us to several general conclusions about campaigns. First, about the only material advantages that are distributed in campaigns are positions in government and certain vague promises to leaders for access and general support of their demands if elected. The election decides who will be in office and who will not be. It is only after the election that specific policies are formulated and adopted through bargaining, compromise, and concession.

Second, the election also helps to determine which groups will have the "easiest" access to public officials. Those groups that provide electoral support will, in turn, have the "ear" and support of the elected official. However, the road to election is strewn with general and vague promises and half-truths. This, as we have attempted to suggest, is in the very nature of campaigns.

The above discussion applies primarily to politicians making appeals to heterogeneous audiences. It is also true in election politics, as in bargaining, that to win requires fashioning a majority coalition out of smaller minorities. Candidates, therefore, will tend to take general and vague stands on a number of issues, hoping in this way to reach most of the groups in their audiences. A candidate's choice of issues will also depend partially upon the nature of his audience. For example, when talking to labor groups, candidates will refer to weaknesses and strengths in labor legislation and attempt to show how they, if elected, will act in such a manner as to reduce inequities. When speaking to Negro audiences, candidates will make general and vague promises of helping them also. The same will be true for audiences composed primarily of businessmen, farmers, veterans, and other groups of minorities. More specific issues will be referred to when a candidate's audience is known beforehand, but a candidate's appeals to these more homogeneous groups will still be primarily about style issues affecting the group.

Most of a candidate's speeches, however, are to self-selected audiences made up of a number of diverse minorities. A candidate's speeches usually are made before public rallies and *ad hoc* groups of people who may know he is going to be in town and want to hear him, or at "whistle stops" on a candidate's tour of his constituency. Radio and television addresses also draw heterogeneous audiences. The more heterogeneous the audience, the more general and vague become the style issues.

Political Parties

Political parties are coalitions of publics and groups, organized to make nominations and contest elections in the hope of eventually gaining and exercising control of the personnel and policies of government.[25] Both of our major political parties appeal to almost all groups in the society for support.[26] We do not, as in some other political systems, have "ideological" parties in the sense that there are differences between the parties over how our government should reach decisions. There is, in fact, a high degree of consensus among most Americans on the question of what kind of regime (that is, form of government) we ought to have. What cleavages do exist between the parties (and even within the parties) are over who should staff the government and, secondarily, what they will do when they get there.

Because there is great social and economic diversity within the United States, and because there are only two major political parties, each party is likely to be composed of diverse publics and groups. The primary goal of parties is to win elections and staff the government. Parties will attempt, then, to appeal to as wide an audience as possible. Since there are no ideological differences to speak of, almost no groups are excluded *a priori* from either party. These considerations have several important consequences: (1) political parties will be heterogeneous in membership; (2) differences within parties are likely to be as great as differences between parties; (3) party patforms are likely to be general and vague; and (4) political parties will tend to make similar appeals (for example, party platforms will be similar).

Party politics is a conglomeration of all four of our decision-making processes. Bargaining is best exemplified by national conventions, where presidential nominees are chosen. Leaders interact with leaders for the purpose of choosing a nominee who is likely to win in the general election. In order to win support for their own candidacy, those in contention for the nomination will make "deals" of various kinds with state party leaders (distribution of positions in government, promises of state aid of various kinds, and so forth). State party leaders will also attempt to get the best deal they can for themselves and their state. Many will have previously come out in favor of one candidate over the others and will work for that candidate's nomination. The payoffs are likely to be large if the candidate wins the nomination and election, but the risks of announcing support early are also great. If the candidate loses the nomination, the winning

---

25 Slightly modified from Austin Ranney and Willmoore Kendall, *Democracy And The American Party System* (New York: Harcourt, Brace and Company, 1956), p. 85.
26 See Anthony Downs, *An Economic Theory of Democracy* (New York: Harper and Brothers, 1957), Chap. 8.

candidate will not feel obliged to be overly indulgent toward the backers of losing candidates.[27]

Party politics has elements of hierarchy, democracy, and discussion as well. Hierarchy is involved in the same sense in which hierarchy is involved in any organization. Some party members have more potential power than others and are able to exercise control over group decisions. This aspect of party politics is especially fascinating at national conventions, where it is often quite important for the leader of the delegation to deliver a "solid" state bloc of votes to the candidate he supports. A divided delegation is an indication of weakness within the state party organization.

Democracy is involved in party politics in the sense that many party leaders are elected either by conventions or by party primaries. This fact places the party leaders in a position of having to bid for the support of party members. However, organizational elements involved in these elections (such as party "machines") make them much less "democratic" and less concerned with the symbolic manipulation of party voters than in general elections. Discussion, of course, plays a role in party politics also in the sense that party members discuss issues and candidates among themselves. In fact, as we have already mentioned (Chapter 4), candidates and party labels are the primary elements in most political discussions, along with style issues.

Party politics, then, has elements of all four interaction systems: bargaining, democracy, hierarchy, and discussion. As such it represents a most interesting political laboratory for the political scientist.

Interest Groups

Organized political interest groups are the outgrowth of similar needs arising from common frustrations among people in similar situations. For example, factory workers live and work in common environments and meet common problems. They are faced with a certain level of income with no guarantee that it will increase. They (like most other people) want more money, better working conditions, and so forth. The use of group tactics, such as strikes, pooling financial resources for propaganda purposes, and other maneuvers that

---

[27] See Nelson W. Polsby, "Decision-Making at the National Conventions," *The Western Political Quarterly,* vol. 13 (September, 1960), pp. 609–620, for a fascinating "logic" of national convention politics.

are possible only in a group effort, eventually are seen as ways in which they will better be able to meet their needs. Joining into larger groups for the purpose of petitioning their government for help in meeting their demands soon follows. Since these groups represent not only votes but financial aid to political office-seekers, interest groups can expect at least a minimal amount of access to those engaged in the formation of public policy.

This kind of reasoning applies to other groups as well. Just as labor unions were the result of workers joining together to better their lot, so it is with farmers, veterans, and ethnic, racial, and religious groupings and manufacturers and business interests of all kinds. And, as groups grow in size and make more demands, it becomes necessary for those with competing demands to organize for the purpose of exerting pressures of their own. Organization breeds organization; largeness begets largeness.

Interest groups provide a vital function for democratic politics. That is, not only do they help to promote the interests of their members, but they also serve as an important link between government officials and the public at large.[28] We have already mentioned, in the previous section on political parties, that parties in the United States are not issue-oriented. The primary purpose of American political parties is to make nominations and staff the government with people who are able to win more votes than their opponents. Parties, in this sense, provide for geographical representation. Since candidates are elected from particular constituencies (congressional districts or states), congressional representation helps to insure that sectional and local interests will be considered in the formation of public policy. Interest groups, on the other hand, provide for functional representation within the populace. They insure that a certain segment of the public is heard with respect to economic, social, and political issues. Such issues often cut across geographically defined districts. Interest groups, then, provide another link between the public and its representatives, a link which is concerned with outcomes on particular issues, and which is very often national in scope.[29]

---

[28] William Kornhauser, *The Politics of Mass Society* (New York: Free Press of Glencoe, 1959), especially Chap. 3.

[29] See V. O. Key, Jr., *Politics, Parties, and Pressure Groups* (New York: Thomas Y. Crowell Company, 1958), 4th ed., Part One, and David B. Truman, *The Governmental Process* (New York: Alfred A. Knopf, Inc., 1951), for excellent discussions of interest groups.

Political interest groups, like political parties, are a mixture of various forms of politics. Bargaining characterizes interest-group activities with government. The leaders of interest groups attempt to satisfy the demands of their members by offering their support and the support of their members to government officials in return for the support of the latter on a particular issue that affects the interest group concerned. Interest-group leaders, to gain leverage with officeholders, not only attempt to persuade congressmen and administrative officials to go along with them, but they also attempt to influence public opinion within the officeholders' constituencies. Many interest groups will attempt to enlist the support of groups in various constituencies who may be sympathetic to their cause for the purpose of applying additional pressure on officeholders.

Democracy is also involved in interest-group politics in the sense that many interest-group leaders are elected by group members. However, as we discussed in Chapter 3, most members of groups leave leadership activities to those few who are willing to take the time and effort to participate in group activities. Hence, the relationship between leaders and members in most interest groups is characterized by hierarchical rather than democratic decision-making.[30] Interest-group leaders (especially in labor unions) have been able to get themselves re-elected time and time again without significant opposition. One-party, rather than two-party, politics is the rule rather than the exception in group life.[31] This fact is due not only to the lack of interest by most group members in group activities, but also to leadership control over communications with members and to the recruitment of new leaders by co-optation.

Hence, interest groups, like political parties, are concerned with the distribution of both symbolic and material rewards. Symbolic manipulation occurs in the leadership's relations with group members at large (as with political parties), and material advantages are primarily distributed in the bargaining that goes on among leaders and other decision-makers outside of the group.

---

[30] See Seymour M. Lipset, Martin Trow, and James Coleman, *Union Democracy* (New York: Free Press of Glencoe, 1956), for a discussion of this situation in labor unions.

[31] Lipset, Trow, and Coleman, *Union Democracy*. See also Robert Michels, *Political Parties* (New York: Free Press of Glencoe, 1949).

7

SUMMARY

AND CONCLUSIONS

Politics concerns the distribution of advantages and disadvantages among people. A discussion of the factors that influence the distribution of "payoffs" has been the central concern of this book. We have grouped these factors under two headings: (1) differences in people and the kind of resources they have to bring to bear in the decision-making process, and (2) the type of decision-making process itself. Payoffs we also divided into two types, material and symbolic. The general model of politics, then, as suggested in this book is as follows:

Independent Variables	Dependent Variables
1. People and resources.	1. Material advantages.
2. Decision-making processes.	2. Symbolic advantages.

In other words, we have attempted to explain the distribution of advantages and disadvantages (dependent variables) on the basis of differences in people and their resources and differences in decision-making processes (independent variables). The summary to Chapter 5 sketches out this model in more detail.

The major conclusion that can be drawn from our analysis is that "politics" is actually a number of different kinds of "games," all going on simultaneously. These games we have classified as bargaining, hierarchy, democracy, and discussion. The outcomes of these games are different because the people involved are different, the rules of playing are different, and the goals of the participants are different. In some games (for example, democratic games) leaders interact with non-leaders for the purpose of winning office. Knowledge of what leaders and non-leaders are like, that is, their values, attitudes, and beliefs, helps us to understand why leaders play the game they do and why campaigns are primarily concerned with the symbolic manipulation of public opinion. Such knowledge also helps us to specify what the rules of the game are likely to be and what kinds of strategies and tactics are likely to lead to success.

Bargaining games, on the other hand, involve a different interaction situation (leaders interacting with leaders); and hence, on the basis of our knowledge about the values, attitudes, and beliefs of leaders, we are able to specify (at least in broad outline) the kinds of interactions that will take place and the kinds of advantages and disadvantages that will be distributed. The rules of the game will be different from the rules of democratic politics; strategies and tactics leading to success will be different; and the distribution of outcomes will be concerned with material rather than symbolic advantages. Hierarchical and discussion games also have their differences in rules, outcomes, and participants.

Implications for the Implementation of Policy Preferences

Knowledge of how our American political system works has several important consequences for the individual beyond the sheer joy of understanding how the system functions (although this is not to be discounted as unimportant). For example, we have defined government as the implementation of public preferences into public policy. We may distinguish totalitarian governments from democratic ones by the number and diversity of public preferences that are taken into account in the decision-making process. Democratic governments (owing primarily to the competitive electoral process and the consequent access to decision-makers) are characterized by the greater extent to which the preferences of publics are taken into consideration in the formation of public policy. Totalitarian governments, on the other hand, place severe limits on the number of publics who are allowed to share in decision-making. This policy obviously affects, in a number of important ways, the manner in which advantages and disadvantages are distributed in totalitarian systems.

First, in totalitarian systems bargaining tends to be less equal and shades quite easily into hierarchy. The official decision-making bodies already have their own conception of what is in the "national interest," and competing conceptions are not allowed. Hence the bargaining that does go on tends to be much narrower in scope and assumes a posture of compliance rather than conflict. Second, those who wish to bargain have fewer resources and fewer points of access to decision-makers. They are unable to attempt to broaden the scope of the conflict to include significant publics. Such channels of communication to the mass public are left, rather, to the official decision-makers. Third, because fewer publics are allowed to participate, there is less of a chance to build significant support among others for your cause. Particular interests tend to be isolated, and hence they find it difficult to build coalitions.

This means, of course, that knowledge of how politics operates in totalitarian countries does not necessarily increase an individual's or group's chances of success in satisfying certain preferences. Only a limited number of preferences are considered legitimate, and these tend to be quite narrow in scope. Politics is much more restrictive in totalitarian systems in the sense that only a narrow group of public activities are allowed, and only a few of the many potential publics are allowed to participate. Knowledge of the American political system, however, because most publics are allowed to participate in the political process, is knowledge that can more readily be put to use for the purpose of satisfying *our* preferences. This is not to suggest that, because we know how the political system operates, our preferences will automatically prevail. It is to suggest, however, that we will have a better chance to get our policy preferences accepted by decision-makers if we know how the game is played and are willing to participate in it.

A second important consequence for knowing how the American political system functions has to do with proposals for changing the rules. As we have attempted to indicate throughout our discussion, the rules of the game help to determine the distribution of advantages and disadvantages. For example, in Chapter 6 we illustrated how the

Electoral College, in the election of the President, tends to over-represent the interests from large, two-party, urban states. Now, if we are in agreement with the policy preferences of those interests, then the Electoral College serves as a rule in the political system that increases the likelihood that our preferences will prevail. If, on the other hand, our policy preferences tend to coincide with the interests of smaller, one-party, rural states, then the Electoral College method of electing the President does not aid us in satisfying our policy preferences.

There have been a number of suggestions, in recent years, to change the method of electing the President. Some prefer abandonment of the Electoral College and the substitution of direct election of the President. Others prefer to keep the Electoral College but, rather than having the total electoral vote in each state given to the candidate with the highest number of popular votes (as is presently the case), to have the electoral vote divided among the candidates in the same proportion as the popular vote. Without going into the details of these proposals, both Electoral College "reforms" would tend to take away the advantage of those interests in large, two-party, urban states. This is just one example of many that could be cited in which the rules of the game help to determine whose preferences will be translated into public policy. For example, the manner in which Congress is elected tends to favor smaller, one-party, rural states.

The rules of the game, then, help to determine who is advantaged and who is disadvantaged. Changes in the rules change the relative advantage of different interests within the population. Knowledge of the rules and the manner in which the rules affect payoffs is there-fore an important datum in the calculation of whether or not the rules ought to be changed. Those who are aware of the effects of the success of getting their policy preferences translated into public policy that changes in the rules would have are therefore in a "better" posi-tion to evaluate proposed rule changes. Whether or not one is in favor of changing the rules of electing the President may be deter-mined partially by the effect such a rules change would have on his ability to have his preferences prevail.

Knowledge of the rules of the game and the advantages given to some groups because of the rules also helps the individual to protect himself against manipulation by others. For example, in most reform proposals to change the manner of electing the President, no mention is made of the effect such a change would have on the implementation of the preferences of various publics. Such rule changes are usually stated in the form of being more "democratic." If one also knows that the question of who is likely to get what out of the political system is also involved in rule changes, he is less likely to be "taken in" by the appeals to "democratic" ideals alone. Such criteria may still be important in his evaluation of rule changes, but they will not be the only criteria.

Many of us have preferences with regard to public policy, that is, we approve or disapprove of increasing social security benefits, we approve or disapprove of subsidy payments to farmers, and so forth. Understanding how the political process works will help us to translate our preferences into public policy. Second, many of us have preferences with regard to how decisions ought to be made, that is, with regard to the rules. Some of us may feel that the President should be elected by direct election rather than by the Electoral College, or we may feel that the President should be given the power to veto specific portions of legislation rather than have to accept or reject legislation in its entirety.

But, as we have attempted to point out in this conclusion, the rules of the political game help to determine whose preferences will prevail. All rules confer advantages on certain publics. Knowledge of the political process, then, not only helps us to translate our preferences into public policy; such knowledge also helps us to evaluate the process itself in terms of our preferences. Government is defined as the implementation of public preferences into public policy. Whose preferences prevail becomes, then, one of the most important questions we can ask.

INDEX

INDEX

250025/284